TOOTS

To Cub & Dana

With affection

Bob Considine

"21" Nov. 7 69

Books by BOB CONSIDINE

MacARTHUR THE MAGNIFICENT
30 SECONDS OVER TOKYO
(with Ted Lawson)
WHERE'S SAMMY?
(with Sammy Schulman)
INNOCENTS AT HOME
GENERAL WAINWRIGHT'S STORY
THE BABE RUTH STORY
DEMPSEY, THE MAN HIMSELF
(with Bill Slocum)
RAPE OF POLAND
(with Stanislaw Mikolojczyk)
RED PLOT AGAINST AMERICA
(with Robert E. Stripling)
THE MARYKNOLL STORY
KHRUSHCHEV
(with W. R. Hearst, Jr., and Frank Conniff)
THE MEN WHO ROBBED BRINKS
(with Specs O'Keefe)
IT'S THE IRISH
PANAMA CANAL
MAN AGAINST FIRE
IT'S ALL NEWS TO ME
TOOTS

KARSH, OTTAWA

TOOTS

by

BOB CONSIDINE

MEREDITH PRESS / New York

First edition

SBN: 696-83921-0

Library of Congress Catalog Card Number: 73-91865

MANUFACTURED IN THE UNITED STATES OF AMERICA FOR MEREDITH PRESS

VAN REES PRESS • NEW YORK

To Husky

. . . with love

bc

Contents

1. *"An outside demon, but an inside angel."* 1

2. *"I don't wanna be a millionaire. I just want to live like one."* 23

3. *"...Put your arms around a millionaire."* 60

4. *"...Thousands of bums will be homeless."* 89

5. *"All I've done is exchange saloons...."* 134

6. *"I never once saw Spelly at the bar."* 143

7. *"You're holding the hand of the President of the United States."* 164

8. *"Dear God, here we go again."* 186

Index 209

CHAPTER 1

"An outside demon, but an inside angel."

BERNARD (TOOTS) SHOR was invented by Abraham and Fanny Shor in South Philadelphia shortly after the turn of the century. No patent was applied for. There could never be another one like him. Some have had reason to consider this uniqueness a break for the human race. They shudder at the thought of more than one Toots Shor. But many feel that if America had hosts of Toots Shors it would be happier, more highly moral, friendlier, more generous, and, as a consequence, broker.

What makes Toots special is that he became involved in an unprecedented era in American history. The thread of his odd life stitched together the people who made much of the history and mood of the 'twenties, 'thirties, 'forties, 'fifties, and 'sixties. He must be the only man who was as close to mob lords Longy Zwillman, Big Frenchy, and Owney Madden as he was to Cardinal Spellman, Robert Sherwood, and President Truman. His personality, outgoing and often as erratic as a rocket, bridged the sociological gaps that yawned between Babe Ruth and Paul Draper, Frank Costello and Edward R. Murrow, Texas Guinan and the nuns at Marymount, where his three daughters were educated. He was equally at ease, and vice versa, with Sir Alexander Fleming, the discoverer of penicillin, and Casey Stengel, the inventor of the new syntax. He served as catalyst between two distinguished Americans, Yogi Berra and Chief Justice Earl Warren.

Since his arrival in New York from Philadelphia in 1930, Toots's surface image has altered. He was first looked upon as a bouncer, then as a greeter, then as a manager, and

1

finally as an owner. Each designation was somewhat wide
of the mark. He was never a bouncer, as such, though he
bounced countless mob guys, souses who dared use profanity
in front of their ladies, and even clouted a few prohibition
agents representing the majesty of the United States Government. He was more than a greeter; he soon had a piece
of the profits wherever he worked. When he was a desig-
nated manager it was largely an honorary title, for he never
quite knew how to manage himself. His position as owner has
been diluted by a variety of more or less silent partners, or
comakers, ranging from a New Jersey movie theater operator
named Leo Justin (whose death plunged Toots into a near-
record mourning binge) to Jimmy Hoffa (whose prosecution
precipitated a temporary rift between Toots and his friend
Attorney General Robert Kennedy).

Actually, Toots has remained Toots, whatever his titles
and places of business. He was Toots through parched
periods of flat-pocket, and Toots through the deliriously
short-lived period when he was a millionaire. Mark Hellinger, his New York discoverer and amused patron, wrote
in his popular column in the New York *Mirror* that Toots was
the "classiest bum in town." Bugs Baer, virtually the inventor of condensed candor, observed, "Toots was a bum in
Philadelphia and all he did was change towns." When Toots
dined at the White House, Bob Hope sent him a wire: "They
put a pig in Tiffany's window."

Toots's most enduring image is that of abuser. ("You
creepy bum. . . . You crummy bum. . . . You crum bum. . . . Get
outta my joint, you lousy, creepy, filthy bum," etc.) However, the ultimate curse he can call down on the head of
friend or foe is puzzlingly tepid.

"He's nothing but a piece of raisin cake," he will say. It
does not do much for the listener. No one has yet blanched
on hearing this seething curse. But it satisfies Toots. It wipes
a man off the face of the earth.

Toots's number-one exclamation, which he finds suitable
for all occasions, is equally sanitized. It is "Jiminy crickets!"

He used it the day in 1965 when he learned that the Archdiocese of New York had selected him to cater the luncheon

for members of the Papal court who accompanied Pope Paul VI on his historic one-day visit to New York, the United Nations, and the World's Fair. It is believed Toots also used the exclamation when two prohibition-era mobsters forced him and a gangster's girl into a warehouse and sicced a gorilla on them.

If a tally had been kept through the years, it would show Toots has taken more abuse than he dished out. In his perpetual duel of give-and-take, Toots has been outgunned frequently by better-armed wits. But he usually winds up on his feet.

His early training could be responsible for that gift. As the only Jewish boy in a predominantly Catholic community, he was given the hard alternative of landing either on his feet or his skull. His early efforts to make friends with the other boys of his age were sometimes rebuffed to such a degree they would chase him home like a pack of wolves closing in on a toothsome rabbit.

In time, Toots learned to outwit them in a novel way. He discovered that by running through any Catholic church in his line of flight he could gain a few valuable yards of open space between himself and his pursuers.

"Those bums would have to genuflect when they passed the altar," Toots recalls, "I didn't have to break stride."

"I remember the day he was born," his gentle sister Esther said of her burly brother not long ago. "In those days women had their children at home. When my sister Bertha and I went off to school that morning everything around the house seemed normal. But when we came home that afternoon Daddy took us into the bedroom and there was Mama lying in bed with Toots in her arms. They told us the stork had brought us a brother.

"He was the most beautiful baby, and the most beautiful youngster. He had long blond curls until he was four. My mother insisted on that. Even though she had always wanted a boy, she dressed him in clothes Bertha and I had grown out of. The first day he wore pants we had his picture taken in his little sailor suit. Later that same day Daddy had Toots's curls cut off. My mother fainted when she saw Toots with a Dutch bob, but we had saved the curls and she had them framed. He was all boy from that time on. 'An outside demon but an inside angel,' Mama would say of Toots."

The mother of the Shors, one of thirteen children, was born in St. Petersburg and brought to America when she was twelve. Deprived of schooling, she went to work as a slavey in a Philadelphia factory to help support herself and her sisters and brothers. Abraham Schorr was born in Leipzig and attended university in Munich. He was of Austrian descent. When he arrived at Ellis Island in the 1880's, some cynical or semi-illiterate United States immigration man spelled his name *Shor* and would entertain no correction. A brother who had preceded him to America took him into the household and taught him the trade of shirtmaking.

Abraham met Fanny Kaufman at an engagement party in Philadelphia and they were married soon after. The year was 1895. He was twenty-seven; she, twenty-two. It is not likely that either had a premonition that eight years and two daughters later they would produce a male child of somewhat unusual distinction: the only former bootlegger and poolshark prodigy who ever hoisted the former King Edward VIII by his royal bare behind in the locker room of the anti-Semitic Seminole Club, Palm Beach. ("I was a little bagged," Toots later said, establishing a new Olympic record for understatement.)

Abraham Shor was a gentle, philosophical man. He taught his lively young wife as would a patient tutor. In time she spoke clearer English than he, an interesting switch on the Pygmalion theme. He retained his German accent to such a degree that during World War I, Fanny told him, "Don't talk too much, or we'll all be arrested as German sympathizers."

When the Shors first moved into a house at 15th and Wharton Street in South Philadelphia and opened a cigar and candy store to supplement the father's meager income in the shirt business, their neighbors threatened to draw up a petition to have them evicted. They were the first Jews in the area. Toots was four years old at the time. One day he burst into the house, winded and crying.

"They called me a Jew," he told his mother.

"Well! What did you say, Son?"

"I told them I couldn't help it," Toots said.

Either by sheer guts, or out of his enemies' admiration of his broken-field running through strategically located Catholic churches, Toots won his spurs with his Christian peers.

His mother contributed.

"A boy hit me," he reported one day, through a puffed lip. He expected to be enfolded in his mother's apron and comforted. But his mother said a startling thing.

"Go out and hit the boy who hit you," she ordered.

He did, thus inaugurating one of the longest—if sporadic— fistic careers since Joe Palooka.

"My mother was a little woman but real strong," Toots says, sprinkling his loving memory of her with repetitions of "God bless her." His memory of his father is a bit different. "He was a wonderful, educated man, tall and well-built but like a Mr. Milquetoast. My mother ran our family. She taught me the greatest lesson I ever had: she taught me to fight."

The acceptance of Toots as a social equal in his dese-and-dem environment took several forms. At nine he was appointed official mascot of the basketball team of St. Rita's Roman Catholic Church at Broad and Federal. Toots is still proud of that.

"We had great basketball in Philadelphia in those days, church league basketball. We had St. Monica's, St. Thomas', St. Theresa's, St. Peter's, St. Rita's, and a lot of others. Lefty Connors, our manager, took a liking to me and so did the players. Somebody asked my mother, God bless her, if she was worried about me, a Jew boy, spending so much time around those Catholics. Mom, God bless her, said, 'I'm not worried; Toots is a good boy.'"

Toots cannot remember who gave him his nickname.

"Maybe an aunt or somebody like that," he says, searching a mind that otherwise has such total recall that he knows the name of the third baseman in the Tinkers-to-Evers-to-Chance infield and the date of President Roosevelt's "quarantine" fireside chat.

"Whoever gave it to me, it stuck," he says, contentedly. "Somebody said to my father once, 'Why don't you stop calling that boy Toots?' My father said, 'He'll always be my Toots.' It's okay. After all, nobody's going to take me for a fairy." (Toots's boyhood chums had more spectacular names: Frisco Legs, Lobster Louie, Siggy, Smiff, Plug, Sausage, and Flatnose Jimmy Kelly.)

St. Rita's added still another facet to Toots. He learned to shoot craps in that holy place's recreation basement.

"It was a good place to play," he said years later. "The cops never raided it."

He learned his baseball in the streets. Street baseball was illegal in Philadelphia, along with bearbaiting and proper salaries for Connie Mack's Athletics. Whenever the cops pounced on the team on which Toots played, he led his one-time pursuers on a beeline to his mother's shop, bypassing all Catholic churches. Once the team had arrived and assembled itself behind Mama Shor it knew it was safe. As the cops entered, Mama Shor would pick up the baseball bat she kept behind the counter.

"If one of you lays a hand on these fine boys, I'll hit you on the head," she would say. "They have no place to play except in the streets."

Toots yearned for the sight of better baseball than he and his newfound chums could produce.

"He'd say to me, 'I'll shine your shoes for nothing if you take me to Shibe Park,'" his sister Esther recalls fondly. "So I'd take him there now and then to see the Athletics. He was crazy about sports, all sports, and that disturbed Daddy. Daddy was terribly smart, but he was a German and simply couldn't understand. He'd shake his head and say it was a waste of time: Toots should study."

Actually, Toots was studying quite hard at that time at Drexel Grammar School, preparing for South Philadelphia High. He was also taking another course in the basement of the Church of the Annunciation at Tenth and Dickinson: pool. The church's recreation room had three tables.

Toots has many fond memories of that portion of his misspent youth.

"One day a bunch of Dago and Irish kids are playing at Annunciation and a priest comes down from upstairs. The priest yells, 'Come on, all you boys up to Mass.' It was some special kind of Mass.

" 'Tell him we're Jews, Toots,' some bum whispered to me. I gave him my big blue eyes and said, 'We're all Jews, Father.' So he blew. He couldn't put us out, so we kept playing pool."

Esther, at that time a yeomanette in the Philadelphia Navy Yard, got wind of her little brother's new interest in life and became both his friend and foe. The roles blended. On the one hand she kept the terrible secret from the other members of the family. It would have been too much for them. The Shors were a loving but well-disciplined household. The children had to show their hands before being allowed to sit down to a meal. Slang was out, profanity unthinkable. Evenings were for mind improvement. Father Shor would read by the hour to Mama: the classics, the great novels and poetry. And here was the youngest of the household, soon up for his bar mitzvah, shooting pool. It was bad enough when he shot it at the Catholic church, but now, with some long pants borrowed from a boy named Leo O'Donnell, he had moved on to a regular pool hall at Broad and Federal.

"I'd make a point of walking that way whenever I had a date," Esther remembers. "I'd send my date into the place to see if Toots was there, but he'd seldom find him. Toots usually posted a lookout, some kid who would spot me coming down the street and yell, 'Hey, Toots, here comes your boss.' And Toots would escape out the back way."

Esther did not tell on Toots until after his bar mitzvah, and then with a heavy heart. She felt she must, for his own sake.

A crisis of major proportions moved her. She learned that Toots had pocketed the fifty dollars his father gave him to give to Rabbi Klein of Temple Adath Jeshurun, Conservative, and had later blown it in a neighborhood crap game. It was one of the first in a long series of spectacular financial deescalations in Toots's gambling career.

Esther told the awful truth to the father in front of Toots. Abraham was stunned. When he could speak, he gave the errant son a quietly outraged lecture at the conclusion of which Toots turned to Esther and said, "I thought you loved me. You're nothing but a fink." Neither she nor the father had ever heard the expression but both regarded it as a great obscenity. Shor ordered Esther to go to the bathroom and fetch his razorstrop. She obeyed. But when he raised it to strike his son, Esther stepped between them. She loved her father deeply, but this was different.

"Don't you dare hit him!" she cried out, and his arm slowly wilted.

Great tragedy struck the Shors on the night of August 29, 1918.

Esther, returning home late from her Navy Yard job, found her mother, her sister, Bertha, and a schoolteacher neighbor, a Miss Stewart, chatting on the Shors's front steps. Esther had a side line at the time; she was a stringer for a South Philadelphia neighborhood paper and was paid a dollar for each accepted story she phoned to the news desk.

"You missed a good bet tonight," her mother said as she joined them. "There was quite a fire down the street."

It was too late to do anything about it, so Esther kissed her mother good night and went to her room. Toots, fifteen, was asleep.

Esther had scarcely reached her room when she heard a screech of braked tires, a collision, and then a shuddering thump against the house. An ambulance, racing down 15th Street, had been brushed by a passenger car driven by a doctor. The ambulance careened off course, headed for the Shor house, jumped the curb, and plunged into the petrified women. Miss Stewart was badly injured. Bertha suffered a broken back. Fanny Shor, who had come such a long way in America, struggling and believing all the way, was decapitated.

The shopkeepers of a neighborhood that had once threatened to banish the Shors, shuttered their windows on the day of Fanny Shor's last rites and procession to Har Nebo cemetery. Boys who had once slugged Toots or chased him endless miles stoned the doctor's home.

"There were fifteen limousines at Mama's funeral," Esther says with quiet pride.

It was a bad turn for the men of the Shor family. Abraham never stopped grieving over his beloved. They had been the kind of couple who holds hands while walking down a street. He visited the grave every day for the first two years after Fanny's death and then, as his health declined, every Sunday for the next three years. His weight dropped from 200 to hardly 125. He wanted no food except milk and raw eggs. He wept a great deal at night.

Toots, now a junior at South Philadelphia High, began cutting classes to give himself more time for his pool hustling. Whenever the school dispatched a note to the elder Shor, demanding an explanation of Toots's absenteeism and threatening expulsion, Esther or Bertha would intercept the warnings. Why add to their father's grief?

The father kept his brood together in an increasingly absentminded way. His heart lay in Har Nebo.

"Hey, Dad, did you ever see a redheaded Jew?" Toots asked at the dinner table one night, breaking the silence and trying to shake his father's reverie.

The puzzled father said, "I don't believe so, Son."

"Well," Toots said triumphantly, "one's sitting next to you."

Esther had hennaed her hair. The father gazed at his daughter for a time.

"Your mother would turn over in her grave," he sighed.

Soon after the mother's death the little store over which she presided so merrily was sold and the family moved to 1611 Porter Street, a block from an up-and-coming boxer named Tommy Loughran, who was to become the light heavy weight champion of the world. It was mostly an Irish neighborhood, and once more there would be trouble.

Some of it was caused by Toots, some of it ended by him.

He and a pal named Gus Vitullo were getting a reputation as junior pool hustling masters in South Philadelphia at such adult parlors as Allinger's and Coward's. Often they were followed by a small army of youths and fellow ne'er-do-wells who backed them with quarters and half-dollars in their contests with resident hustlers. Their skill led to occasional fights with outraged losers, sometimes with lethal cues. It was a happy period for Toots. On a good day or night he might make as much as six dollars.

Toots's father roused himself from his mourning on the Thanksgiving after the death of the mother. He asked Toots to remain at the table after the girls left.

"Are you going to school?" he asked.

"No, sir."

"I've known it for about three weeks," the father said.

"Then why didn't you tell me?" Toots asked freshly.

His father hit him for one of the few times in his life.

Toots's sister Bertha, by now a teacher, interceded with the principal of the high school and Toots was reluctantly reinstated. His school work improved steadily through the winter months.

"But spring got to me," he says now. "Gus and I went back to hustling. Still, I passed the final exams and finished my third year. They were sure sore at me for passing, because of all that bagging I did."

The trouble that Toots settled about that time had a familiar ring. His sisters told him that their father had been having trouble with some neighborhood toughs when he would return home from a visit to the cemetery. Their house on Porter Street had been vacant for some time before the Shors moved in, and its steps had become a meeting place for the hooligans.

"Yesterday when Daddy came home one of those fellows said, 'We're not moving for any Jew,'" Esther told her brother.

"Next day I made a point of being home for a change when Dad came home from the grave," Toots recalls with relish. "I stayed inside, peeking out a parlor window. Sure enough, the same thing happened. I busted out of the house and, well, I guess I fought like the Jews in Israel. I really beat those guys up, three or four of them.

"But now I was in the same fix in the new neighborhood

as I was as a kid in the old. But I got a lucky break. Jimmy Kelly, as good a street fighter as I ever saw, and a pal of mine too, had also moved into this neighborhood. Joe Gilmartin too. Like Jimmy, I had grown up with him.

"Well, they walked home with me from the pool hall at Broad and Federal the night after I had beaten up those tough guys. The guys I had licked, and a few more, were waiting for me, naturally. But when they saw Kelly and Gilmartin with me, nobody touched me. From then on they became my friends and I became theirs."

Toots was seized with an ambition to become a professional fighter about that time. Philadelphia was alive with good young fighters and many boxing clubs thrived. He was convinced that his friend Kelly would be an outstanding pro. How could he miss? Kelly had flattened a bigger fellow with a single punch when the guy had said something disparaging about Toots, behind Toots's back. ("That taught me something, a code I've lived by ever since," Toots says piously. "Nobody knocks a friend of mine when he ain't around.")

Kelly did enter the ring at that time but was no match for somewhat older and much more skilled fighters. Toots was not discouraged. He raced home one day to tell his father excitedly that none other than Jack McGuigan, head of the National Boxing Club, had offered him seventy-five dollars to fight a preliminary.

Abraham Shor looked solemnly at his son and heir.

"If you ever fight for money, don't come home," he said.

Today Shor likes to say, "I guess the only time my father enjoyed seeing me fight was the day I licked those bums on our front steps."

At sixteen, Toots told his father he wanted to quit school and go to work. The father would not hear of it; Toots must have an education. Toots came back with another proposition: "If I can pass a college entrance exam would you let me work? That would mean I could always go to school later, or at night while I'm working." The father nodded.

Toots attended Drexel Institute, took the college boards and managed to pass by a hair, helped by his good memory. The following day he went to work for an electrical company as a timekeeper. It did not last long. Toots's cousin, Joe Karr, owner of the Eclipse Shirt Company, offered him a job in the stockroom.

That was the birth of Toots the clothier. He entered his new work with zest and Karr moved him here and there in the firm to season him for bigger things to come. When he was nineteen he became an assistant to the vice-president in charge of informing clients by mail just how many orders Eclipse could or could not fill. Toots did the research.

"I enjoyed that more than anything I ever did," the world-famous pubkeeper recently observed. "I got so interested I went to the Wharton School of Business for a year, studying correspondence and English. But I don't like to talk about that. I wouldn't want people to think I was educated."

Toots became the man of his family on June 15, 1923, a month after he had turned twenty. That was the evening Abraham Shor, more brokenhearted than usual, did not return home from Har Nebo. He went instead to a cousin's home, and there he took his life.

Esther had always been the apple of his eye. He had rocked her to sleep each night until she was into her teens. But it was Toots the cousin called by phone to break the news. He was at work at Eclipse. He gave a few instructions as to funeral plans, then went home to tell his mature sisters. He told them their father had been killed by a trolley. There were laments in the neighborhood that night, and more the next morning when the *Inquirer* carried the real story.

The remaining Shors moved into an apartment. The sisters went about their respective jobs, schoolteacher and clerk, and a bigger job they felt they now had to undertake: looking after Toots.

Shor was a chore.

He immediately gambled away the $1,500 which each of the heirs was bequeathed in the father's will. So the sisters put up $200 each and provided him with a fresh stake. He blew that too. The dice were cold and the pockets (the pool tables, not Toots's) too small. He developed champagne tastes but his cousin-employer would pay him hardly enough to buy beer.

"I gave him a hundred dollars to buy a suit for his twenty-first birthday," Esther recalls fondly. "I was visiting in Pittsburgh at the time so I wired birthday congratulations to him at the apartment. I addressed the wire to Mr. Bernard Shor. The next day Western Union notified me that it had been unable to deliver the wire, so I anxiously put in a call to him. Yes, a telegram had arrived okay, he said over the phone, 'but no Mr. Bernard Shor lives here; only Toots Shor.' Then he said, 'And by the way, Sis, you owe me ten dollars.'

"I reminded him tartly that I had already given him a hundred. 'I know,' he said, 'but I also bought a hat, a ten-dollar straw hat.' "

Esther chuckles over the memory, then adds, "He was all boy."

Toots became a host and *bon vivant* on his sisters' salaries. They never knew just when he might roll in for dinner with half a dozen friends from the shirt factory or pool hall, all famished.

"Some mornings, a lot of mornings, he'd say to me, 'Do you have change for a ten, Sis? It's the smallest I've got,' " Esther recollects. "I'd say, 'Look in my purse and see if I do; I don't think so.' So he'd look in my purse and I'd have five or six dollars, let's say. He'd say, 'Well, a man's not going to marry you for that kind of money, or take advantage of you.' So he'd take the five and leave me the one.

"We'd go out to dinner once in a while, on the lunch money Bertha and I had saved. We'd go usually to two restaurants, 1919 Chestnut and the Reading Terminal. Toots would insist on being the one to pay the bill at the cashier's place. We'd slip him ten dollars, say, and notice that the bill might have come to six or so. We'd ask for the change, but Toots would have none of that.

" 'Give the change to the waiter,' he'd say to the cashier. And when we complained he'd wave our arguments aside. 'That poor man has to live, doesn't he?' And that would be that."

Among other gifts Toots received when he became twenty-one was a set of studs from his cousin Joe Karr.

"For your tux," Karr said.

"I don't have a tux," Toots said, blushing. So Karr sent him
to one of the better stores in Philadelphia and suited him up.
He looked magnificent in it, so fine that Karr announced he
was going to buy him a membership in the exclusive Philmont
Golf and Country Club. Toots turned it down.

"What would I want to belong to Philmont for?" he said to
his benefactor, who had also become his guardian after the
death of the elder Shor. "Jeez, I'd have to leave all the kids
I was raised with. I don't know any of those guys out there.
They're all rich. Sorry."

Karr was a patient man. The next year he appointed Toots
as a salesman and gave him South Philadelphia as his beat.

That was the birth of Toots the salesman. He found it an
ideal occupation. During the baseball season that year he
would sell shirts through the morning and early afternoon.
At two thirty he dropped his sample case, for safekeeping,
at the pawnshop owned by one of his uncles, and then went
to the ball park. He had moved out of the apartment by now,
after an argument with Bertha, so there were no longer any
ties that bound him to hearth and home. Fanny Shor had said
of him at thirteen, "Wait'll he gets the smell of a girl. They'll
never let him alone." Toots, the boy salesman, proved her to
be an astute prophetess.

Not all of his early romances were serene.

During one sojourn at Atlantic City Toots served temporarily as a lifesaver. He stood more than six feet tall, weighed
170, was fair of head, rosy of jaw, and was shaped like Max
Baer.

"Toots had one drawback as a lifeguard, he couldn't swim,"
George Jessel will tell you. "But he saved many a life. When
he saw a guy drowning he'd stand on the beach and yell out
to him to swim in immediately or he'd come out there and
bust him one. Gave a lot of drowning men the shot of Adren-
alin they needed to save themselves."

Toots had an eye for half the girls on the beach and, if he
is telling the truth, all the girls had an eye for him. But one
superbly designed blond amazon particularly caught his
fancy that season. And vice versa. Five minutes after meeting
her, Toots extracted a promise from her to go out with him

that night at the end of his exhausting day's work of sun-bathing. When she was out of earshot, but still a vision in white silk bathing suit, Toots bragged about his conquest to another lifeguard. The man's tan suddenly bleached.

"You can't do that, Toots," he said with horror. "That's Rocky's girl."

Rocky was the unassailable boss of that part of Jersey and all of its shady citizens. His very name stirred terror.

Toots made a sound like "ptuie" and beat on his chest, just like Elmo K. Lincoln, the first of an unnerving series of Tarzans.

"To hell with Rocky," Toots boomed. "Tonight she's *my* girl!"

"You could be killed, Toots," the man said, thoughtfully.

Toots chose a mob-type nightclub as the scene of the great rendezvous. As he and his beautiful statuesque date entered, a man got up from a table and threw a right-hand punch. It hit the girl on the jaw, which was the puncher's intention.

Toots floored the assailant with a left and right, pulled him off the deck and stood him up against a wall.

"You damn fool, you could be killed!" he said to him tensely. "Don't you know she's Rocky's girl?"

"Yeah," the guy said. "But she's also my wife."

After two years with the Eclipse Shirt Company Toots had what he calls a "dee-bate" with his patron Karr. He joined the B.V.D. company and moved to Wilkes-Barre, company headquarters.

"I'd work Scranton, Pittston, Williamsport, Reading, Lancaster, Harrisburg, Carbondale, Pottstown . . . far as Altoona," he remembers. "But after getting to know the managers of those stores and sometimes even the owners, I'd call 'em on the phone. I'd call a fellow in Williamsport, say, and I'd say, 'Hi'ya, Joe. I've got some new items.' I'd describe them and he'd give me an order. Then I'd get out my road map and figure the mileage from Wilkes-Barre to Williamsport and back and charge B.V.D. seven cents a mile. The guy who hired me knew what I was doing. He had done it himself."

B.V.D. expanded Toots's sphere. It considered him a crack

young salesman and he was. It sent him far afield from Wilkes-Barre to sell and to attempt to break a growing practice by clothing stores to sell B.V.D. men's underwear for 99 cents instead of $1.25 in order to lure additional trade. On the road, and he worked Illinois, Iowa, and Nebraska, Toots would augment his never enough salary (or blow it) by hustling the local pool hustlers.

Even though Toots was given the enviable privilege of selling the first B.V.D. bathing suit—an honor he still treasures— he quit the company after two years. He was road sore. Besides, one of his girls had wired him collect that she missed him and please come back to her. There were other extenuating circumstances. His cousin Dewey Kaufman owned a nightclub in Atlantic City, the Beaux Arts, and gave Toots a weekend job as a cashier during the summer of 1929. It afforded him time to run a little booze, hustle a little pool, and display his manly charms on the beach.

"I liked that job," he says in retrospect. "Dewey, the best nightclub man I ever met, paid me more than I was making with B.V.D. and had enough confidence in me to put me in charge of the waiters. So I quit B.V.D. It was amachoor night, that job, compared to working in Atlantic City. Some of the prettiest girls in the world worked down there in those days. Every laid-off chorus girl in New York would come down there in the summer and go to work at a club, making fifty, sixty dollars a week. The clubs drew the top acts in show business, a lot of them still working today."

Toots returned to Philadelphia when the 1929 season ended. He lived for a time with two friends in an apartment at 23d and Walnut. He describes that period of vagrancy as "fooling around, going to nightclubs every night, laughing. Hustling pool was the only way I could make a dollar."

Toots's friends moved and he lost his pad. He could not in good conscience return to his sisters' flat.

"I didn't have a place to sleep for a couple of nights but then I moved into the apartment of a friend named Ben Street, a bookmaker—a beautiful apartment. Ben used the apartment only from two o'clock in the afternoon until seven.

So I began sleeping there, but I had to be out by noon—when they'd come in to get ready to make book."

Toots drifted happily into 1930. "He went broke *before* the stock-market crash," his friend Joe E. Lewis says of him.

"Then one day I'm back down in Atlantic City in my uncle's saloon, uncle Bill Kaufman, one of the greatest saloon-keepers I ever saw," Toots says, setting the stage for his favorite story. "Pop, they called him. Dewey's father. Pop always spoke with a dialect. Newspaper guys loved him. He had quite a few saloons, one near the Philadelphia *Ledger* when it was going.

"So, while I'm sitting there at the bar in his Atlantic City place, Pop came over to me and looked at me and my drink.

" 'You're a bum,' Pop said. 'You'll never be nothing but a bum.'

"I looked at him. There was no use giving him an argument. So I quickly got up, walked a block to the bus station, and took a bus to New York."

ABOVE: Toots's mother and father, Fanny and Abraham. BELOW: Toots, at four, contemplating the impending loss of his curls. OPPOSITE PAGE: Toots the Life Saver, hoisting Willie Mosconi above the sands of Atlantic City. They had cultural rapport. Mosconi was the uncle of the greatest pool player in the world.

Toots and Baby are married at City Hall by Judge Hines, November 2, 1934.

ABOVE: Leon and Eddie's on a swinging night—with Leon Enken, Helen Morgan, Eddie Davis and Baby, and a guy who just sat down. BELOW: A night out at Leon and Eddie's: Toots's mother-in-law, Mrs. John Volk, Jackie Gleason, Baby, Toots, Bert Lahr, Eddie Davis and Leon Enken (standing), Fred Finkelhoffe, Nicky and Mrs. Blair

DAVID WORKMAN

Toots and a treasured sparring mate, Quentin Reynolds

CHAPTER 2

"I don't wanna be a millionaire.
I just want to live like one."

TOOTS's first meal in New York after accepting exile from Philadelphia was in Bickford's, which he remembers glumly as a "one-arm joint."

"I had on a brown suit, can you imagine that?" he asks incredulously. "And brown shoes!" He makes it sound as if he were Columbus apologizing for discovering the New World with soiled sails on the *Santa Maria*.

However, Toots was soon living it up in the most exciting town in the land. And without any visible means of income. It was a good time to arrive in New York, solvent or busted. The personality of the expatriate mayor, Jimmy Walker, pervaded the post-Wall Street crash. A deflated boomtime millionaire would still occasionally take a dry dive out of his overdue-rent downtown office or uptown penthouse. There were soup lines, and the advance platoons of apple venders.

But, like Walker, it was a town that lived one day at a time and wrung everything out of the twenty-four hours involved. It had never been tougher, more gay or optimistic. A white reveler and his beautiful girl could barrel out of the Cotton Club and walk the streets of Harlem in the dead of night and never dream of experiencing trouble. Central Park was navigable without police escort. The only war then raging was the one between the mobs which owned the speakeasies and the revenue men whose job ostensibly was to shut them down. New York was Chicago under the Marquis of Queensberry rules.

Toots fitted the picture like a frame, though he was flatter than a slice of liver. Happily, he was adopted as a guest—

tenure uncertain—by a cousin, Jack Cohen, and another boyhood chum from Philadelphia, Rudy Weiss. Cohen and Weiss worked for the New York office of Warner Brothers Pictures and shared an apartment on West 55th Street. They were highly successful young men. In sharp contrast to their jolly guest, they had it made.

Cohen earned $25,000 a year as a lawyer for the film company; Weiss was in its prestigious real-estate division. When they decided to move to Central Park South's glittering Essex House, they took Toots along for laughs.

The move prompted Toots to give vent to a bit of warped philosophy which Clifton Fadiman and Charles Van Doren saw fit to preserve in *The American Treasury—1455–1955.*

"I don't wanna be a millionaire. I just want to live like one," Toots said. In time the remark shared a page in the anthology along with Franklin D. Roosevelt ("These economic royalists complain that we seek to overthrow the institutions of America"), with Henry Ford ("Fortunes come. They are not made"), and with Daniel Webster ("Failure is more frequently from want of energy than from want of capital").

Cohen introduced Toots around the town. He narrowly escaped being hired by Joe Bernhart, Weiss's boss in the realty division. Had the job come through he might have blown his niche in American folklore. Safely past that hazard, Toots was then more or less deposited in the lap of Joe Moss, operator of Broadway's thumping Hollywood Restaurant. Moss didn't have any work for him at the moment. So he introduced him to John Steinberg and an associate simply known as Christo. They ostensibly owned and ran the 5 O'Clock Club on West 54th Street between Sixth and Seventh Avenues. They hired Toots for fifty dollars a week to smile and handle the fights.

The real owners were Owney Madden and Big Frenchy. The manager of managers Steinberg and Christo was Sherman Billingsley, a bootlegger who later became the host-darling of café society.

Madden was a quiet little man who never had to raise his voice. In the realm he ruled, his word was the law. Big Frenchy, whose name was George La Mange, was a breezy ham-fisted enforcer of the Madden Law. Billingsley, who had come East from Enid, Oklahoma, was a suave and efficient general manager of the mob's fashionable speakeasies.

Toots was one of the smallest cogs in the organization, but he loved his work. He basked and beamed in the presence of the 5 O'Clock Club's patrons: Florenz Ziegfeld, Harry Richman, Bing Crosby, Jimmy Cagney, Eddie Dowling, and other luminaries.

"All caviar men," he says of them, reaching for the ultimate tribute. He speaks at much greater length about the girls who would drop by the club to kid around with the big blue-eyed yokel from South Philly: stunning girls from the *Follies,* George White's *Scandals* and Earl Carroll's *Vanities.* Billingsley was not amused. *He* had been the one the long-stemmed beauties flirted with, not some bum named Toots who had to sell an occasional case of whiskey to augment his meager salary.

Toots's education advanced the hard way:

"I'm only there a week or two when a girl I knew from Atlantic City comes in with a fellow I didn't know. I okayed him on account of her. So they walk over to the bar and he says he wants to buy a bottle. I sold it to him.

"He just let it set there and looked at me. 'She tells me you're a pretty nice fellow,' he says. 'You look okay to me too. So I'm giving you some advice: don't ever do what you've just done. If I took a drink out of this bottle you just sold me, it could mean your job.' He turned out to be a fellow named Lou Sutton, a revenue agent. He had me cold, just when I figured I had found the best job of my life. 'So watch it,' he tells me. A real decent bum."

A week later another agent "made a buy" and there was commotion in the place. Big Frenchy was summoned by phone to rush to the club. He was an acknowledged master of the art of "talking" to any agent who was determined to padlock a place. If this did not work, Big Frenchy had a touching alternative—cash.

Toots had an even more direct approach. Noticing that the agent had taken the evidence with him when he went to the men's room, Toots went in after him, picked an argument with him, and in the ensuing scuffle broke the bottle.

"Now he's got no 'buy,' see?" Toots recounts in happy retrospect. "So the guy blows without making a pinch and everything is calmed down by the time Big Frenchy arrives. The guys tell him what I did and he looks me over.

" 'I've heard about you,' he says. 'Why don't you come see me someday?' "

Toots gave his leader a bright hard smile.

"When I come to see you, I want to make money," he said. The syntax was somewhat wanting, but Big Frenchy seemed to understand.

Toots began feeling he was part of the in group of the empire. In addition to the 5 O'Clock Club, the mob ran the Napoleon Club, once the queenly town house of Mrs. Woolworth Donahue, Zelli's, and the flagship of the scofflaw fleet, the Park Avenue Club. Billingsley, in addition to overseeing those establishments, owned and operated his Stork Club.

"The Park Avenue Club was the class of the group," Toots muses. "It was the most expensive place around. It had a circular silver bar—that's where I got the idea for my own round bars. It was run by George Lamaze, one of the last of the great gourmets. We all looked up to George. He was a graduate of Brown University, imagine that. He wound up running the Warwick Hotel in Philadelphia for Jerry Louchheim. There was nobody like George. When you talked to him it was like talking to, let's say, the first guy to bring out salad bowls."

Toots remains sentimental about the 5 O'Clock Club.

"Just think, I met Bing Crosby and Bob Hope for the first time there. Bing was on radio, sponsored by Uneeda Biscuits, how about that? Hope was in vaudeville. J. C. Flippen was one of the most popular guys around. So was George Burns, Georgie Jessel.

"I was a lucky bum. Hellinger and Corum took a liking to me. Wherever they'd go, they'd take me along with them. It was like later when Crosby and Hope used to fight for the company of another bum, Barney Dean. Hellinger and Bill Corum taught me how to stay broke. They were the biggest wheelers and dealers with money I ever saw. Hellinger was the strongest check-grabber I ever knew in my life. He and Bill showed me how to have a good life. They had to be the two most important newspaper guys in town.

"Mark would take me to the seats I now have at Madison Square Garden, when it was the old Garden. There would always be a lot of tough guys in the ringside seats in those days. When they'd see me walk in with Hellinger and sit by him, I was okay with them. Hellinger was the best-liked guy among the hoodlums who ever lived. Why? He was straight and honest with them and he liked to talk their talk. They could trust him. I remember when he broke his leg, his hospital room was filled with flowers from Madden, Charlie Sherman, Dutch Schultz... everybody. Everybody loved Hellinger, including people like Jock Whitney—those kind of people too. It was the same with Bill. Wherever he sat it was the head of the table."

After three or four months at the 5 O'Clock Club, Toots got the heave-ho.

"One day when I come to work there's Steinberg and Christo waiting for me. They had bum news: Billingsley had ordered them to fire me. 'He don't want you around,' they said.

"It was tough. I liked being around with all those beautiful girls and meeting all the top theater and film people. I used to write home to Bertha and Esther: 'You'll never guess who I saw tonight—Adolph Menjou!' Or 'Saw Walter Winchell.' 'Saw Mark Hellinger.' 'Saw Bill Corum.'

"Now I was out, all on account of Billingsley. I guess maybe our chemistries didn't hit."

Eddie Dowling, the director, saw to it that Toots was soon reemployed. He introduced him the next night to Tommy Guinan, Texas's brother, who was managing the Napoleon Club. Tommy suggested that Toots go home, put on his tuxedo and report for work immediately. It tells something about the chemistry of Toots that, broke, he told Guinan he couldn't make it until the next night. Toots had a date.

Toots was back in fistic action sooner than he expected. On one of his first nights at the Napoleon he was tipped off

by the doorman that a known revenue man was trying to
get in. Toots went outside and flattened him. Then he went
back to work, which he describes as "a greeter, a host, you
know; fighting different guys. The thing outside, when I got
lucky and flattened this guy, was extra."

Madden himself was soon on the phone.

"You the fella . . . ?" Madden asked him.

"Yeah."

"They're getting out a body warrant for you. Why don't
you get out of town? Draw a thousand dollars."

It was one of Toots's proudest moments, and for a time he
was speechless.

"Where do you want to go?" Madden persisted. "How
about going down to see George?" George La Mange, Big
Frenchy, and assorted corrupt Cuban officials owned Orienta
Park, the Havana racetrack.

Toots said he'd prefer Philadelphia and Atlantic City: "So
I went back with the biggest score I had ever had. A thousand clams! I'd walk into some little joint either in Philadelphia or Atlantic City and buy a drink for the house. Drinks
were maybe forty cents a shot and there wouldn't be more
than thirty people in the store. For twelve or fifteen dollars
I became a big shot. So I'd go to some other joint and order
another round. If anybody asked me who'd bankrolled me,
I'd just say, 'Owney Madden and I are like *that*,' and leave
'em for dead. So how would the bum who asked the question
know that I had only spoken to Madden on the telephone?
Once."

Toots and his fortune were soon parted. The body warrant
heat was off too. So Toots concluded that if Madden & Company had given him a thousand dollars to go away, they'd
give him a couple hundred to come back. He figured correctly, and was back on the job at the Napoleon when he
received a call from Madden. For Toots, it was like yesterday:

"Getting called by Madden in those days was like being
called by the President. So I went to see him, of course. He
had an office in that theatrical building at Forty-seventh and
Broadway. He looked me over for a long time. He was a little

guy, about the size of, say, Lou Ayres or Davey Marr, the golfer. Thin."

Madden finally spoke: "You think you're pretty tough, don't you?"

"I'm as tough as anybody you got around here," Toots said. "Bring your best man in."

Madden liked his furniture too much.

"Sit down," he said.

Madden grilled Toots at some length. It was one of several searing examinations made of him at that time. On one occasion Eddie Dowling, who also wished to know as much about Toots as possible, invited Toots to accompany him to a penthouse on Central Park West.

"I want to introduce you to some nice fellows," Eddie explained.

Toots was greatly impressed by the splendor of the lobby, the fast-rising elevator, and, above all, by the apartment itself.

Its main room was a soundproof shooting gallery. An effigy of a man was painted against the bulletproof rear wall. Three or four killer types used it regularly for practice with live ammo. They didn't like strangers, glared at Toots as he entered, put their guns back in their holsters and left. When they were gone Dowling explained, while watching Toots's changing expressions, that he had told them that Toots was a very tough new guy in town, ready for anything—including a demonstration of how he, too, could hit the dummy on the knee, elbow, or between the eyes.

Toots had never fired a gun in his life.

One afternoon Toots was having a drink at the Kentucky, Seventh Avenue and 46th Street, with a girl-about-town whose current number-one man was a tough mug named Nettie. Soon Nettie and a fellow mobster walked in, ordered drinks, and stared bleakly at Toots. Then Nettie came over to their table.

"Let's take a little ride," he said, and added, "if you got the guts." That was calculated to bestir Toots and it did. Nettie and his friend drove Toots and the girl to a warehouse on the Lower East Side. They bolted the door, told Toots and the girl to stand where they were, and then they opened a large cage. Out stepped a gorilla and advanced on Toots and the screaming girl who was clinging to him. Toots got set to take what he felt would be the last punch of his life. But just then Nettie hit the monster on the head with a baseball bat and it walked meekly back into its cage.

"Just wanted to see what you'd do," Nettie said with grudging admiration.

The tests continued.

"One day at the Napoleon I'm sitting down with Frenchy and about five or six fellows. In those days you wouldn't know whether guys like that were actors or hoodlums; they all looked alike. All built like Ben Hogan. Well, a tough guy comes along and says, 'Okay, you guys. Everybody away from the table.' The five or six guys get up immediately and leave. I just sat there.

" 'Who's this?' the tough guy asks George. Before Frenchy could answer I said, "I'm as tough as you are, that's who I am."

" 'Some kid just come up from Philadelphia,' George says.

"The guy looks at me for a long time and then he says, 'Will you go with me?'

"I looked at this bum and said, 'Anything you do, I'll do.' "

The tough guy took Toots to Harlem and they went from place to place, drinking. He never once spoke to Shor, not even during a fight Toots had with two patrons in one of the places. After several hours he whistled up a cab and the two returned to the Napoleon Club. Big Frenchy was still there, waiting.

"He's okay," the tough guy said, "but don't let him go to Harlem."

Toots's assessor was Jerry Sullivan, one of the toughest men of that exotic era. He was Madden's and Big Frenchy's "lieutenant." He enforced their laws as he saw fit.

"He became my friend, which was good," Toots says. "In those days you could get killed and nobody would know it, or where you were planted. There would be nobody to write to my sisters in Philadelphia. It was nice to have a friend like Jerry. It was protection.

"The same with Johnny Broderick, the detective. He was so tough Jack Dempsey tried to hire him as a bodyguard. I was in a fight one night in front of the 5 O'Clock Club. I'm about to take this guy out when one of his friends steps in. Now I gotta fight two at once.

"Suddenly I hear somebody say to the new guy, 'Stand back! One at a time!' It was a real order. It was Broderick. He had been watching the fight in the crowd. When it was finished, he came up to me." It went like this:

"You're all right, kid," the legendary Broadway cop said.

"Thanks," Toots said coolly, and long later explained, "I didn't have too much love for a cop in those days."

They became inseparable friends.

"Broderick became my one-man gang. He always gave me good advice. For example, he'd say, 'Fight 'em with your hands.' The old George Raft and Edward G. Robinson pictures you see on the 'Late Late Show' make a big thing out of prohibition gun battles. Sure, those guys carried pistols, or most of them did. But during all that period I never saw anybody shoot anybody. They were more interested in handling booze and beer. Having a brewery was as strong as having a gambling house. Madden, Frenchy, and Bill Dwyer owned the Flanagan-A brewery. I don't remember what the percentages were, but they all lived big and spent money like anything. King Beer was owned by a guy named Levy. Maybe Dutch Schultz had a piece of it. There was a lot of beer in Jersey: Max Greenberg, Waxie Gordon, and I imagine Lucky Luciano had pieces of that action.

"They didn't go to war much against each other, like Chicago. Before I got here, there was a war about to start but Jimmy Walker sent for Madden and asked him to stop the war. 'It would hurt the city,' Jimmy said, so Madden called it off. One of the few tough guys nobody could trust was Vincent Coll. He was nuts. He was out to kill everybody in Dutch Schultz' mob because his brother Pete had been killed by one of Schultz' guys. Schultz, Marty Krompier, and other partners stayed up in the Bronx for a couple of years, afraid to come downtown because Coll was here. Whoever called him 'Mad Dog' Coll nailed him pretty good."

Toots has mixed memories of the Napoleon.

"I was kinda under the outside doorman, Tom Barry. Muscle-bound sort of guy. Couldn't fight a lick. But a good man. In those days an outside man *had* to be good. He had to know people, know who to let in and who to keep out. It was a tough job. I was Barry's assistant, inside. A greeter, and slugger. Maybe the whiskey was different then. You had more arguments in a place than you have today. Some of the people with money, in those speakeasy days, would become very foulmouthed, cuss a lot. They'd cuss checkroom girls, cigarette girls. I'd say, 'Hey, cuss the people you're with, not the help.' If they kept it up, I'd flatten anybody.

"A fight in those days could begin with a guy getting fresh with a girl, let's say. Or two guys would get in an argument and you'd have to go in and split 'em out. Or one guy would pick on *you*. It was like 'an apple a day keeps the doctor away.' You'd have a fight a day. Nobody seemed to care. Nobody seemed to beef. Next day the guy you fought the night before might be around the place, having a drink, and you'd figure, well, he just had a bad night.

"It was too good to last. One night I'm working in the Napoleon—Frenchy and Madden were out of town—when the bookkeeper came over to me and told me I was through. Billingsley was sitting in the next room, and I knew he was the one who gave the order.

"They owed me one hundred and sixty dollars. I went up to the cashier—Billingsley's brother-in-law—and said I wanted my money now. He looked doubtful. So I walked behind the bar, punched a key on the cash register, took the hundred and sixty, and put it in my kick and left."

Toots had a good time not working in the wake of that particular disaster.

"Hellinger was out every night on the town and he'd go looking for me. I made myself easy to find. We'd eat at Moore's, go to three or four nightclubs a night, wind up at his place, 180 East 79th . . . parties every night. What a time!

"Charlie Sherman, a tough guy, was a friend of Mark's. He owned a speakeasy on Fifty-fourth between Sixth and Fifth, near the Ziegfeld Theater. He wanted me to be the manager.

Offered me two hundred dollars a week. I had never heard of two hundred a week. He said I'd be the big boss of the joint and anything I said would go. All on account of Mark, of course."

Toots bravely turned down the attractive offer.

"I thought to myself, well, every night I'm out with Hellinger, going to the best places in the town. Why should I go to work? If I go to work, I can't have this much fun. I explained that to Hellinger and he just laughed. That's when he wrote that column calling me 'the classiest bum in town.'"

In time, a press-agent friend of Walter Winchell's, Mark Bachman, got Toots a job at the Ball and Chain, a speakeasy at 52d and Park Avenue. Toots is still indignant.

"Couple guys named Gransky and Weiss owned it. They had heard a lot about me and were so sure they'd get some new business out of me that they cut me in for ten percent of the business. It was the first place where I got a piece of the action. Sure enough, some of the actors and girls I met at the 5 O'Clock Club and the Napoleon began coming in and business picked up real good.

"But Gransky and Weiss were no-gooders. Somebody tipped me off that I wasn't being cut in on ten percent of the joint's slot machine. So the night I found that out—the place was crowded—I walked over to the machine, waited for my turn to play, then picked it up and slammed it down on the floor. Then I picked it up and broke it over a table. Naturally, I blew that job.

"It was the first time I was out of work in New York without a shove from Billingsley."

Work caught up with Toots after a spell of "walking around ... hustling." He ran into an independent speakeasy owner named Charlie Lucas. They had met on Toots's first night at the Napoleon and had discovered they had one great thing in common: both hated Billingsley. On that occasion, after Toots got off work, Lucas took him to a party in his Duesenberg.

"Girls and booze all around," Toots recalls fondly. "I wrote home to my sisters: 'What a spot this is, New York. If this guy Lucas can do it, there's no telling what I can do in this town.

I'll own everything in this town within six months or a year.'"

Lucas put Toots to work as an assistant manager at his Maison Royale, 10 East 52d Street, in the fall of 1931. Shortly thereafter, Lucas opened the Montparnasse next door. It was the classiest place Toots had ever seen.

"Everybody had to wear a tuxedo. It was the first speak-easy that gave people publicity for showing up. You brought your own booze. It had acts like the Yacht Club Boys, which was the hottest act in town then; they got eleven hundred dollars a week. Tony and Renée DeMarco danced there; six hundred dollars a week. Emil Coleman's orchestra played, for maybe one thousand dollars a week. The Vance Sisters sang for an opening act.

"On opening night everybody was in white tie and tails. Charlie was a stumpy little guy. His tails cost him maybe two hundred and fifty dollars, but they came down to his ankles."

The Montparnasse prospered, but the Maison Royale was padlocked by revenue agents just before Christmas, and that meant Toots was out of a job again. It was embarrassing. He had been writing his sisters in Philadelphia that he was doing great. Now he borrowed $500 from Lucas and sent each of them $250 for a Christmas present to carry out his boasts.

Lucas generously offered Toots 25 percent of the cut to come over to the Montparnasse, but Toots could not bring himself to accept it.

"Charlie was a gin drinker," he recalls grimly. "He would have wanted to run it. *I* wanted to run it."

So now he was out of action again, but his special guardian angel, surely one of the more overworked seraphs of that period, fluttered forth:

"I'm sitting in some club when Eddie Davis came in. Some-body said to Eddie why didn't he hire me. Eddie and Leon Enken, his partner, were building a new joint at 33 West 52d. They'd been at 18 West 52d before that. Jack White took over that place after they left and had the best show of its kind we ever had in New York—with guys like Frankie Hyers, Pat Harrington, and Jackie Gleason, all working for peanuts."

Eddie, a first-rate Broadway impresario, put Toots to work

as day manager of the rowdy, wonderful place where, years later, the present Toots Shor would rise. It was sheer bliss:

"I was in charge from noon till six. It would be jammed with women. All of my friends' wives would come in and have lunch there. Val Ernie's band played through the afternoon.

"I was getting maybe seventy-five dollars a week and a certain percentage over what they figured they should take in during an afternoon. With that I was averaging maybe one hundred and twenty dollars. But at six on the nose, Phil Davis, Eddie's brother, used to growl at the cashier, 'Take that tape register off,' meaning off the cash register. Jiminy crickets, the joint was packed by then and they'd all be *my* customers.

"So, anyway, I'm gambling there, gambling good, and sometimes I'd make book too. Jimmy Collins, the doorman at Twenty-one, got me started on that. He was booking and making a fortune. So I figured if he can do it there, why can't I do it here? I was making book, holding the action, and gambling besides. Leon was a big horse bettor. He'd give me a stub . . . what he wanted to bet on in this or that race. I'd put it in my pocket and never lay it off on another bookmaker. That's what's called 'holding the action.' Leon never had a winner anyway, so what difference did it make who he paid? He'd pay me, and I had never put the bet in."

Toots struck it rich. He could hardly lose anything he bet on: horses, fights, baseball, football. In a dizzyingly short time he had more than $300,000 deposited in the Warwick Hotel branch of the Underwriters Trust. Now he could live like his hero Mark Hellinger, once described by Rudy Weiss as a man who figured money was just cards "made to deal out."

Emulating Mark carried with it certain responsibilities, like switching from rye and ginger ale to brandy-and-soda. Mark had married Gladys Glad, Ziegfeld's top show girl a few years before, so it was only a question of time before Toots would marry a show girl. The odds were that he would choose the type he was so often seen with in his earlier days in New York: big, durable, outgoing girls who could crack plaster with their laughter and take it and give it with equal heartiness.

It did not turn out that way at all. Marian Volk, called Baby by everybody except Toots, who calls her Husky, has averaged about one third of her husband's weight for most of their thirty-five years of marriage. But from the start she has managed to control him through good times and bad like a deft trainer sending a docile elephant through its act. Toots met Baby by chance.

"I invited a big good-looking dame named Iris Adrian— redhead—to have dinner with me one night at the Maison Royale. She shows up okay but she's got this kid with her, Husky. She was sixteen, lots younger than Iris, but she already had a place in the *Follies'* line."

When Toots and Baby began going steady the following year, by which time she was in Earl Carroll's *Vanities*, Toots's chums around Leon and Eddie's and elsewhere razzed him for "robbing the cradle." Hellinger did not join in. One night Toots and Baby were at a place Nicky Blair, one of the fabled men of Broadway, was running at Valley Stream, Long Island. Hellinger strolled over to their table.

"You're going to get married," he said to Toots.

Toots said, with customary bluster, "Are you kidding? I'm never going to get married."

Mark said, "You're going to get married, Tootsie, and this is the girl."

And she was. When Baby went on the road in 1934 as the second lead in the Sam Harris–George S. Kaufman play, *Bring on the Girls,* starring Jack Benny, Toots decided he had to have her around all the time. He took her to Philadelphia to meet his people, Jews who worked faithfully at their religion, and she showed him to her devout Catholic parents, John and Ethel (O'Shea) Volk. Baby inherited her lively sparkle and doll-sized figure from her Irish-born mother; her deep religious faith from her father, a teetotaler who later managed Toots's whiskey cache at his restaurants and turned out reams of rhymed prayers and supplications. The Volks adored Toots. The Philadelphia Shors, Kaufmans, Karrs, Weisses, and Cohens loved Baby. There were several million fond allusions to "Abie's Irish Rose" within the families and among their friends.

They were married in the fall of 1934 at City Hall by a judge who was a brother of the then most powerful politician in New York, Jimmy Hines. (They were remarried at St. Patrick's Cathedral some years later after the birth of Bari Ellen, first of their four children.)

The City Hall marriage was front-page news, at least it was in the New York *Journal.* It was the paper of two of Toots's best friends, Bill Corum and Bill Farnsworth. The colorful city editor, Amster Spiro, splashed page 1 with a nice picture of the ceremony in the judge's chambers.

It took Toots almost a year to lose his $300,000 plus. He will never forget his tender first wedding anniversary, November 2, 1935.

"I'm still working at Leon and Eddie's but I'm not there. I'm at Twenty-one listening to the radio. It was the day Ohio State, the best college team in the country, was playing Notre Dame. I was broke but a bookie—one of Sam Boston's guys—took my bet of ten thousand dollars on Ohio State. Francis Schmidt was their coach. My friend Elmer Layden was coaching Notre Dame. At half time, Ohio State's leading thirteen to nothing. Now the bookmaker's calling me up, offering me fifteen to one, twenty to one to hedge off on some other bets. I growled. Why should I hedge on my bet? I've got the strongest team in the country and I'm leading by two touchdowns.

"Well, you know what happened. Notre Dame started moving. They scored once and missed the goal. Now I'm thirteen to six. With maybe a minute to go they scored again, but missed the try for extra point and I'm home free, thirteen to twelve. I walked out of Twenty-one and took a deep breath and went someplace to have a drink. Well, I'm there drinking and celebrating when some guy walks in and says Notre Dame scored on one of the last plays of the game and beat me eighteen to thirteen. I remember my first wedding anniversary from that. How about that Schmidt! He put in all his subs near the end, so's they'd get to play, and that's why he lost. That's why *I* lost."

Toots got in an argument with Leon not long after that and either quit or was fired. He was broke and out of work but his bookies continued to carry him, sometimes as high as thirty thousand dollars. His friends stuck by him and, in his odd way, he by them. His pal Joe E. Lewis returned about that time from Hollywood after making a picture with Loretta Young. Toots and he had met in the early thirties when Toots was temporarily at leisure and Joe E. was working at the King's Terrace, where Gallagher's is now on 52d Street. Joe would class Toots up by sending a champagne bucket to his table with the napkin covering its contents, a couple of beers. This would induce people in the joint to believe Toots was back in the chips again and was not looking for a sizable touch. They'd send over drinks to Toots, and Toots and Joe E. would return the compliment by drinking them.

When Joe E. returned from Hollywood he called Toots and Baby and asked them out for dinner. During the meal he proposed that the three of them go to Atlantic City the next day for a week's vacation. Toots said, "I can't Joe. I'm tapioca ... tapped out." That was no excuse in Joe E.'s mind. He pulled a roll out of his pocket—it turned out later to be about seven hundred dollars—and said, "I've got this; we're going." Toots (and Joe) remember it vividly.

"So the next day we get in a train and we go. Joe rents a two-bedroom suite in the Ritz-Carlton. I could remember the day when I was a kid when I wasn't even allowed to run on the Boardwalk in front of the Ritz.

"The first night we go to Phil Barr's Five Hundred Club. Phil was probably the most popular nightclub owner who ever lived, among actors. Joe gets a big hand when we walk in. Phil puts us at a ringside table and I'm feeling good. I'm tapioca but enjoying myself. I start sending champagne here, booze there, making friends. Well, after a time they start clapping for Joe E. to do his act. He must've been on the floor for an hour. They wouldn't let him go. But finally he sits down, has a drink, and calls for our check.

"The captain comes over and says, 'No check, Mr. Lewis. Compliments of the house.' So I say in a loud voice, 'Give us the check!' And I turn to Joe E. and say, 'Joe, you can't be obligated to Phil Barr. I certainly wouldn't want to be.' And I say to the waiter, much louder, 'Give us the check!' All the time Joe E. is saying to me, 'Please . . . please.'

"So they give Joe the check. It's for about four hundred.

"We went home the next day. Joe E. wanted to shoot me. So did Husky."

Being broke had one consolation after Toots left Leon and Eddie's. An assistant manager of the Underwriters Trust took him severely to task for blowing the $300,000-plus nest egg. His stern reprimand had Toots's head hanging in shame. But not for long.

"Two months later this bum who gave me hell was pinched for embezzlement. Blew it on some blonde. It was mostly money deposited in his bank by Fred Allen and Jack Pearl. They were a couple of guys who might sometimes make eight, ten thousand dollars a week. They'd deposit it and never take nothing out. So this creepy bum figured their dough was easy to tap, and that's what he did until he got caught."

Toots still gives a listener the shaky feeling that losing his $300,000 plus was worthwhile, so long as the embezzler who lectured him was done in.

Toots's next job offered some unusual financial benefits. It was at the House of Morgan, named not for J. P. but for the lachrymose singer of the same surname, Helen. The place at 54th and Madison was built as a tribute to the star by Harry Kannen, a freewheeling Broadway figure whose money came from a string of gas stations. He was stuck on Miss Morgan, to put it lamely. Toots was named manager. One of his jobs was to pick Miss Morgan up when she would fall off her piano, bombed.

Kannen had two silent partners, Big Frenchy and Lucky Luciano. Toots was close enough to them to call them by the names that only their intimates used: George and Charlie, respectively and respectfully. Their association with Kannen and his infatuation with Miss Morgan gave Toots an idea.

He went to Luciano and said, "Geez, Charlie, you put five grand in this new joint and Kannen names it after *his* girl. What's wrong with *your* girl? He's got a lot of nerve doing a thing like that without checking with you. Do you want me to get your five grand back?"

Lucky nodded. "You got something there, Toots. Sure, go ahead and get that money for me." Toots went to Kannen.

"What's this?" Kannen demanded indignantly.

Toots shrugged. "He wants it back, Harry. Give me the dough and I'll give it to him."

Kannen said the hell he would cough up the five.

Toots looked at him. "Do you want *Charlie* to come over here and ask you for it?"

The thought of dealing directly with one of the more sinister figures of his time was too much for Kannen. He peeled off five thousand dollars and Toots—the genial intermediary—was on his way.

On his way to Belmont.

When that roll evaporated, Toots tried the same story on Big Frenchy and it worked once more.

"Charlie and George knew what I was doing," Toots reminisces happily. "They didn't care. Money meant nothing to either of them. They knew I needed it for gambling."

Kannen now owned the House of Morgan exclusively, but he made the grave mistake of acting the role of proprietor. This offended Toots.

"The place starts doing a real good business, but then Kannen began standing there in front of me, giving the people the big 'Hello, how-dee-ya-do' bit. One night it got too much for me. I growled at him: 'Sit back there in the back where you belong; I'm the manager around here!'"

Toots was, too. He had been delegated great authority and, through his good management and judgment, the place prospered. One of his better coups was related by his treasured friend Sidney Piermont, the famous booking agent, not long before the latter's death.

"One night I'm sitting in the Versailles listening to a sad story from the two guys who ran it, Nick and Arnold. They were griping because there were no new acts around town. All the joints and the hotels were rotating people like Jessel, the Tony DeMarcos, Cross and Dunn, and acts like that. Finally I told them I had seen a new ventriloquist named

Edgar Bergen and I thought he'd be great for their place. They thought I was nuts. Who would listen to a ventriloquist in a nightclub? But they'd give him a tryout. So I got in touch with Edgar's agent, fellow named Jack Mandel, and Edgar showed up the next night with not only Charlie McCarthy but a new dummy nobody had seen before, Mortimer Snerd.

"Well, he killed the audience at Versailles, but not Nick and Arnold. They didn't think he was funny. So I was sitting there with Edgar and Jack—it was like a wake at Campbell's—when Paul Small, the agent, dropped by. I told him our trouble. He got up and went to a phone, called Toots at the House of Morgan, and Toots said to come right over. Bergen went right on the floor at the House of Morgan and knocked them dead. Toots signed him up for two hundred and fifty a week. That's where Rudy Vallée saw him and put him on the air."

Toots's range of friends grew wider, and one of his final nights at the House of Morgan, New Year's Eve, 1935, he saw a fight that he still rates as one of the finest of his lifelong interest in assault and battery.

"The place is packed, everybody in evening clothes. Suddenly I hear a fight outside. Sam Thorpe is working as the doorman. Three guys are after him. Sam knocked them out bing, bang, boom. Three guys! Now he starts for a fourth guy and I run for him and yell 'Sam! Cop!' But he couldn't stop the punch. He hit the cop and knocked him right on his can. How he could punch!"

Kannen did not share Toots's enthusiasm over the great event. They argued "over a hundred dollars, or something," Toots says of that particular loss of a job. And Toots was on the chilled beach again. The remainder of that winter was Toots's toughest layoff.

"Now I'm out of work, married, and we're living at 120 West 58th, paying sixty dollars a month rent. Baby's not feeling well, and one day a marshal showed up with a 'paper.' He was going to put us out. I owed two months' rent. He was going to take the key and throw us out! It was too much, so I said to him, quiet, 'You try it and I'll murder you.' He didn't try it."

About that same time Toots, who had so recently before that had had more than $300,000 in the bank, owed $400 to a shylock named Baxter. One night he was walking home late to the place on 58th Street when he noticed a shadow in a doorway. Two professional strong-arm "collectors" jumped him, to give him a going over. Toots managed to deck both of them. He arrived home showing his wounds but on a note of triumph. He had come to a major decision while engaged in the savage bare-knuckle duel: he would never pay back Baxter, an unusual fracture of Toots's code of ethics. He also wrote off another shylock, one Terry Reilly, for trying to bull him into paying him back $300, plus $60 interest-usury.

"You had to be tough *not* to pay in those days," Toots says of the era. He denies that he ever plunged into self-recrimination over having blown his sizable fortune.

"I just lost it," he philosophizes comfortably. "I won it, so I can't scream about losing it."

Toots scraped bottom until the spring of 1936 when, with the help of Hellinger and others, he latched onto the best job he ever had as an employee: Billy LaHiff's Tavern, 158 West 48th. During the late twenties and early thirties it had been the home-away-from-home of Mayor Jimmy Walker, Ring Lardner, Gene Fowler, Walter Winchell, Ed Sullivan, Corum, Hellinger, and the sports crowd. LaHiff died in 1934; his son had no particular interest in the place and it had run far downhill when Toots breezed in as manager around the start of the 1936 baseball season. He moved Baby and himself into the largest of the several apartments on the top floor of the three-storied building and soon filled the other apartments— at least most of the time—with needy friends. He came to regard it as a personal affront if any good friend who patronized the place tried to pick up a tab.

The day Toots went to work at the Tavern he borrowed three hundred dollars from a shylock to pay off his rent at the little place on 58th Street. And with his salary, percentage, and easy access to the cash register, Toots felt the only decent thing he could do to repay a generous Providence was to start gambling again. The fever hit him big, as usual. He bet on anything that ran, jumped, or swung. He won sixty thousand dollars betting the baseball Giants that season when they won the National League pennant under Bill Terry. He worked hard at the Tavern too. Jack Spooner was its best waiter when Toots arrived. If patrons were unable to get a table handled by the elegantly affable Spooner, they were inclined to go elsewhere.

"So I made Spooner a captain. I put a black coat on him, so's he could be all over the joint, not just at a few tables. I did it. I thought of it. It was my idea and my idea only. Well, there was this guy Will Berstein—good customer—but he kept telling everybody that Spooner made the place, not me. So one day I went to Berstein's office. I walked in and started pulling the drawers out of his desk, like I was going through them. He came in while I'm doing it and yelled, 'What the hell are you doing?' I said, 'Listen, you come in my place every night and tell me how to run my business. Now I'm going to tell you how to run yours.' He never bothered me from then on."

By the time the World Series between the Giants and Yankees opened in October, 1936, Toots had fifty thousand dollars in the bank. He bet it all on the Giants and got odds of 8 to 5. The Yankees won, 4 to 2. (Terry, for reasons still confusing to Toots, didn't follow Toots's generously offered advice on which Giants pitcher to use in which ball park.)

The setback would have dismayed a lesser man. But Toots looked upon it as a victory, with pyrrhic overtones: "I hedged off pretty good near the end of the series. I don't think I lost more than twenty or thirty thousand."

He probably lost more. He was flat when he received an urgent call from his friend Jackie Gleason.

Gleason, busted in Baltimore after a nightclub act of his had flopped, phoned Toots collect and said, "Clam, send me a thou." Toots resembles a beached whale more than a clam —except to Gleason. Toots didn't have a thousand dollars or anything resembling it at the moment, so he made the mistake of asking, "What do you want it for?"

Gleason was insulted.

"I don't need it so bad you have to ask me what for," he

said icily. "And by the way, since you're so nosy you might as well send me two thou." Which Toots did, somehow.

Toots's financial operations in general would have puzzled Ponzi. Sorely in need of five thousand dollars to replenish the Tavern's till, he took dead aim at an old Philadelphia friend, Ike Levy, one of the founding fathers of the Columbia Broadcasting System. Toots set the stage with one of those ominous "I'd like to see you at your office in the morning" phone calls. Then he took an evening train to Philadelphia to get a good night's rest before facing if not his Maker his comaker. But upon reaching his old home town Toots remembered that Joe E. Lewis was appearing there in a nightclub. Toots dropped in for what was intended to be a nightcap.

"First thing I know we're in a joint where B. S. Pulley was playing," Toots remembers through the fogs of time. "It's five or six in the morning. Joe and I walked out, feeling no pain. There's a milk wagon standing there. Joe handed the driver fifty or a hundred and we climbed on the wagon and Joe took charge of the horse. We drove around town past some of my old hangouts. It's now broad daylight so Joe drove me down the busy street where Ike had his office."

Ike was in. It had to be among the swiftest financial transactions on record.

"Hello, Ike," Toots said, rolling in, "I don't need you."

Then he went back downstairs, got on the milk wagon, and Joe E. drove him to Penn Station and put him on a train to New York.

It was all too much for Billy LaHiff, Jr. He offered to sell the place to Toots, who by now was often betting more money on sports events each day than the restaurant grossed. Toots went to a friend of his in Philadelphia, Paul Harron, a realtor, and Harron staked him the modest sum young LaHiff was asking for the lease, something just under $25,000. Harron also gave Toots a 50 percent ownership and, of course, retained him as manager.

With one hand on the pulse of the sporting world (and the other hand in the till) Toots made gambling history around New York. Everybody marveled, except Harron. Just before Christmas, 1938, Harron pried him loose from the perpetual hearty party in the place and said, "Toots, this is outlandish. We can't go along this way much longer. Tell you what I'll do: I'll give you two thousand dollars and you and Baby go down to Florida for a vacation for a couple of weeks, and then when you get back I think you should look around for something new to do—somewhere else." Toots remembers it like yesterday.

"Sid Piermont and Jimmy Cannon happened to be in the place that night so I went over to them and said, 'Well, I guess I'm through with this joint, so let's get some caviar and champagne and live it up.'" The caviar and champagne came to the table but just then Toots got a call from Johnny Boggiano, at the Versailles. Johnny told him that Harron had just been in there and offered Johnny his half of the Tavern. That made Toots mad. He thundered, "Listen, I'm keeping this place!" Then he went back into the dining room and looked around. There were Sid and Cannon, just starting in on the caviar. Toots said to the waiter, "Take the caviar off the table!"

But Toots couldn't swing the dream. He went home with the two thousand in his pocket and told Baby a lie.

"I told her we were going to Florida for a couple weeks' vacation. But I kept stalling and blew the two grand. Then Harron claimed I owed him twenty-five hundred. I went down to Philadelphia to see him and ask him why he'd put out a story like that about me. He was sore at me; I don't know why. He said, 'One day there I wanted to hit you over the head with a plate.' I said why didn't he, and he said, 'Well, I knew what you'd do to me.' Finally he was going to sue me for the twenty-five. I told another Philadelphia friend of mine, Leo Justin. Leo said, 'Toots, I'm going to pay the twenty-five hundred for you. I hope it teaches you a lesson for the rest of your life.'"

(Toots accepted the kind offer but it did not mellow him toward Harron. Some years later Toots's daughter Kerry was in a coma for fifteen hours. Toots prayed with great fervency: "God, I'll do anything You ask me. I'll be nice to everybody, I'll talk to everybody, except two people." Baby heard him. "What's this about 'two people'?" she demanded.

"When you pray to God you got to go a thousand percent."
Toots said tearfully, "I did as close to a thousand percent as
I could, Husky. I only left out Billingsley and Harron. If
I ever told God I'd talk to them, He wouldn't believe me.")

Toots's last night at the Tavern was, traditionally enough,
New Year's Eve, 1938. That suited him. January 1, 1939,
was to be a busy day for him, listening to the three Bowl
games on which he had bets. He won two of them and
started out with three thousand dollars. It lasted a week
or so—a good week or so. Then Toots and Baby moved in
with her parents at their small apartment on West 54th.
The Volks made them feel like visiting royalty, a rare switch
on the in-law bit. But Toots found it rough.

"It's tough to be broke when you're married," he has many
times since remarked. "When you're single, it's easy. You
eat a hot dog, sleep on a park bench. Nothing to it. But when
you're married, the girl you're married to don't deserve that
rap." (Mrs. Shor has never in her life slept on a park bench.)

Toots's friends stood by him during that troubled year of
1939, when they could find him. He spent most of the summer at the New York World's Fair, when he wasn't at the
ball parks or the fights. His spirits were seldom low for very
long. Something would always turn up. One night, however,
he was alone in a strange bar and feeling very sorry for
himself. He felt a tap on his shoulder and turned around
half angrily. He didn't want to see anybody.

It was Johnny Broderick, the detective.

"What the hell do you want?" Toots said to his friend,
belligerently.

"Nothing," Broderick said. "I've been looking for you.
Thought you could use this." He put a big roll of bills on
the table next to Toots's drink and left.

Toots was offered a dozen high-paying jobs during the
summer. He had been around town for nearly a decade and
knew just about every big restaurant owner and beer and
whiskey wholesaler. He had a host of friends who could
be counted to follow him wherever he chose to take a job:
nationally known athletes, theatrical stars, radio personalities, playwrights, fighters, horse owners, and sportswriters.

To the distress of some of his friends who took it on their own to find the right spot for him, he turned down all offers.

Toots had something else in mind, something that only he and Baby and Corum were confident he could pull off.

In the meantime he'd live off his fat and resourcefulness.

"I'm walking the streets," he likes to say of that glum period. "And while I'm walking, I had a dream. I had a dream of building a place. How many guys have a dream of building a place? The World's Fair was on at the time. I'd get in the subway and ride out there every day and just walk around. I was offered a couple of things there: Teddy Hayes, Dempsey's old trainer, was in charge of the United States Pavilion. He was always trying to find a good spot for me. But I'd say no. It would cut down on my walking around and thinking about this dream.

"At night I'd be sitting at the Paradise bar. All those rich guys would come by and say 'Hi'ya, Tootsie,' and give me a shot on the back. But nobody ever said, 'Have a drink,' or 'How about some dinner?' I missed Mark."

Mark Hellinger had gone to Hollywood by that time and was doing well as a producer-writer. He asked Toots and Baby to come out there and stay with him; even offered to build them a house. Toots is sure to this day that he could have done quite well in that odd world. But in turning down Hellinger's invitation he wrote, "Give me one more year in New York, Mark, one year. That's all I want. If I don't come up with something big in one year, I'll come out."

As the summer of 1939 wore on, Toots's dream began to take on substance. He had been alerted by his friend Horace Stoneham, whose New York Giants office was on Sixth Avenue, that the venerable elevated that clattered above the street was going to be razed, which would instantly increase property values in the neighborhood. With the help of George Horn, a real-estate man, Toots homed in on a desirable restaurant site, two old brownstones, 51 and 53 West 51st, opposite Radio City Music Hall. The property was owned by a hardheaded realtor named Charles F. Noyes, Toots was even harder headed:

"Noyes didn't know the el was coming down and nat-

urally I didn't mention it to him when George Horn took
me to see him. He hadn't had any action out of the property for some time, so he offered to put seventeen thousand
five hundred to tear down the brownstones and start my
place. He also gave me a lease for twenty-one years for
some ridiculous price, I think it was a thousand dollars a
month. And I could pay off the seventeen-five over nineteen years.

"Well, the first thing I did was say to George Horn,
'George, you'll get a lot of dough for your real-estate com-
mission, right?' George said, 'Toots, I won't take my com-
mission for a year or two, so you take it now and get your
place started.'" Horn advanced Toots four thousand dollars.

Toots believed with characteristic optimism that he could
tear down the brownstones, dig a foundation, and erect the
basic structure of a two-storied restaurant for $32,500. A
builder named Cohen, recommended by Noyes, assured
him he could. Toots began the great hustle. Bill Corum
suggested that he seek the financial support of either of
two wealthy friends, Tom Yawkey, owner of the Boston Red
Sox, or Frank Stevens, prominent caterer at ball parks and
racetracks. Toots would have none of that. He told Corum
that he "owed" it to Leo Justin to borrow the money from
him. After all, Justin, in chiding Toots for tapping Harron
in the Tavern deal, had said to him, "Toots, why didn't you
come to me instead of going to Harron? Next time, come
to me." Toots was right. Justin and his four partners in a
string of New Jersey movie houses advanced him $15,000
and immediately thereafter another $35,000.

The lease was signed September 15, 1939. Toots will never
forget that date: Lou Nova fought Tony Galento in Philadelphia that night. Corum had invited Toots to accompany
him to the fight but in the rush of last-minute particulars
about the lease, Toots couldn't make it.

"I started walking home to tell Husky about the lease.
I was tapioca, maybe two bucks. I went by a bar Irving
Sherman had just opened and blew the deuce. Well, all
we had at the apartment was some cold cuts. No whiskey.
Husky and I scrounged around and came up with a buck

in change. So I took her in a cab down to the Paradise and we lived it up big. I had a strong pencil there. All the time, Nova and Galento are fighting in Philadelphia. I remember the signing of the lease from that. Galento punched him all over the place, and Tony had been up half the night before."

Toots's hustling was far from done. He talked kitchen-equipment dealers into letting him have what he needed for peanuts down and a dubious but solemn pledge to pay the rest when he could. Foundation diggers hit hard rock which cost Toots an added $7,500 to root out. The money came in the nick of time from the hat-check and washrooms concessionaire. But food-and-drink people constituted serious obstacles. He had given some of them a harrowing time while running the Tavern. Toots needed a new image and he found it in an intriguing way. He called on his friend Eddy Duchin and made an interesting request: would Eddy be a good guy and sign a blank check for him?

Duchin, one of the more successful band leaders in the land, said he'd like to know just how much Toots planned to write in when he got around to filling out the check. Toots said that he couldn't really say. But Duchin signed nevertheless.

"I didn't sleep for a week," Eddy laughed later. "But then Toots came back with the check." It had served its purpose. He had waved it before the noses of meatmen, boozemen, chinaware people, plasterers, plumbers, whatnot—and it had worked like a magic wand. They gave him what he wanted.

As the days inched on toward the completion of the place and the opening of its doors, Toots was offered much free advice on how to win new friends and how not to antagonize old ones. He was selective about the counsel he accepted. When it was first suggested to him that he put nobody on the cuff, no matter what degree of palship or personal fame was the case, his first instinct was to reject such heresy. What would be the sense in having a joint and not feeding and watering his friends? What was friendship *for?* Then one friend played the ace on him. "Toots," he said, "Sherman Billingsley has me and my wife and a lot of other columnists, radio and theater people on the cuff.

He won't let us pay a quarter for all that food, whiskey, champagne, perfume, and red suspenders. You want to try to copy him?"

That did it, Shor thundered. Everybody in his joint would pay.

Toots's ethics held up well in one of the darker hours before the dawn. One day at a sports party at Dempsey's, then located on Eighth Avenue across from Madison Square Garden, a writer said to him, "Toots, you ought to have some cards printed saying you're going to open on such and such a date, and hand them around when you're at a party like this."

Toots was shocked.

"Hand out my cards in another guy's saloon?" he asked aghast. "Never!"

Toots and Justin got around to formalizing their partnership only a week or two before the opening. Such was their faith in their friendship. Justin proposed that they be fifty-fifty partners with Toots in complete control of the operation. Toots balked only at the latter part of the proposition.

"I shouldn't be allowed to handle money," Toots said, coining one of the great truisms of the century. "If a friend asks me for money and I got it, I can't say No." Justin insisted that Toots alone must sign the partnership's checks. Toots would not budge. So it was agreed that both must sign the checks or the checks would not be valid. Justin had gained certain knowledge of how Toots did business and had learned not to shake perceptibly when Toots would go into action. Notably, there was the case of the three bids submitted for the woodwork contract. Toots and Justin went to architect Irving Scott's office to open them. One was for $14,500, another $15,000 and the third, submitted by Charles Froelich, was for $16,000. Though hard pressed for money at the moment, Toots promptly chose Froelich's bid. As they were leaving Scott's office, Justin scratched his head and said, "Geez, Toots, why did you take the highest bid?"

Toots was surprised.

"Because Froelich was the only guy showed up in person," he said. "That means he must be interested." It turned out to be a wise, even clairvoyant, choice of artisans, aside from the beauty of the woodwork and paneling. Froelich in time made an all but unprecedented gesture in the annals of his trade. He didn't ask for all of his money until long after the place had opened.

Curiously, there was a problem about the name of the new place. Justin presumed it would be called Toots Shor's or just plain Toots Shor. Though no shrinking violet, Toots demurred. He appealed to three close friends for advice.

"Why not name it just Toots?" movie executive Grad Sears suggested. "It's got romance." Toots was pleased but not convinced. He sampled elsewhere.

Bill Corum said, "You know, Toots, when you were in the Tavern you got a lot of publicity, but fifty percent of it was Tavern and fifty percent went to you. So why not let it be all Toots?"

The clincher was his talk with Steve Hannagan, Indiana-born but the epitome of the fast-moving, successful New York public relations expert and man-about-town. Hannagan occupied a unique position in the saloon set of those days: he was a good friend of both Toots *and* Billingsley.

Toots tells the story with what must be the same demeanor as Queen Elizabeth II explaining to her subjects why, after much soul-searching, she named Britain's grandest new ocean liner *Queen Elizabeth 2.*

"I told Steve I wanted to name it The City Room or something like that, for the newspaper guys, you know," Toots says. "Or The Projection Room, for my moving-picture guys. But Steve said, 'Why not call it The Stadium, for your baseball pals?' He said it sarcastic. 'What does the Stork Club mean—a baby?' Now he's arguing, fighting me. 'Don't you think Billingsley would like to have his name on front? And what's Twenty-one—a blackjack game? Don't you think Kriendler and Berns would like to have their names out there? The Stork and Twenty-one were speaks that kept their names even after repeal. You're starting fresh.'

"He talked me into it. I told Justin the place would be called Toots Shor. If I had given it any other name, it would

never have been anything but a saloon owned by Toots
Shor. This way, I've gotten all the publicity."

Completed, it cost $141,000—Toots's greatest hustle, until
then.

April 30, 1940 was split into a day and a night to remember. It started on an ominous note. The restaurant
workers union struck the place a few hours before it was
scheduled to open. Sweating, Toots scrounged all morning
putting together a nonunion crew. He had things in hand
by 1 P.M. By some osmosis known only to Toots's set, a few
friends appeared at the closed doors for a drink: Truman
Talley, head of Fox Movietone News, Broadway and night
club star J. C. Flippen, Henry Dunn of Cross and Dunn,
who had worked the old Maison Royale when Toots was
there, and Sidney Piermont.

Toots was ready for them. He had persuaded a bartender
named Red, who had quit Twenty-one, where he had enjoyed great popularity and security, to join him in the
uncertain new venture. Toots offered Red a better deal
than Twenty-one ever did, from Red's point of view. Toots
couldn't pay him any more than Red was already getting
at Twenty-one but he would drink with him after hours,
which his more elegant former employers would not dream
of doing. In time Red "abused the privilege," as Toots says
when passing sad judgment, and he was dropped. As was
his custom, Toots fired him through a middleman. Having
been fired so many times himself, mostly because of Billingsley, Toots could never steel himself to fire anybody
personally.

All the preopening tipplers insisted on paying for the first
round of drinks at the place that was to become the New
World's combination of the Mermaid (where Ben Jonson
and his friends hung out), the Boar's Head (where Shakes-
peare's militant Falstaff downed ale), and the Falcon (show
biz). They compromised and flipped coins. Talley won the
honor. He paid for the whole round with a five-dollar bill
—a commentary on the economics of the day—and all cere-
moniously signed their names on the bill.

Toots went back to the Volks's flat later in the afternoon.

He shaved, showered, and shined while Baby was getting into her best dress. A little after five o'clock Jimmy Cannon, the bachelor sportswriter who was so close to them he was virtually their ward, came over to the flat to pick them up.

When they were ready to go, Toots, on the biggest night of his life, picked up the phone he had installed in his part of his in-law's apartment to call his place.

"I'd better tell them I'm coming," he said to Cannon. He tapped the telephone hook for what became an embarrassingly long time.

The phone had been cut off.

They walked from 54th to 51st Street. They paused briefly outside the two-storied neo-American Colonial building, culmination of Toots's rugged, tumultuous, and spendthrift life. His name was big and bold on the building. The noises from inside sounded like money being spent. It drowned out the pickets' chants. Toots looked at Baby and Cannon, then dipped into his pocket and pulled out all he had—a quarter, dime, and nickel. He threw the coins across the street to the gutter of Radio City Music Hall.

"Aw," he said, "I might as well walk in flat-pocket."

Mayor Fiorello La Guardia takes returned Supreme Commander Dwight D. Eisenhower to the Polo Grounds, at the invitation of Horace Stoneham (far right). Toots and Quent Reynolds are there—

also, to the left of Ike, Winthrop Aldrich and James Lyons, president of the Borough of the Bronx

ABOVE: Group of noncombatants at 1946 World Series in Fenway Park, Boston: Joe DiMaggio, Toots, George Raft and Leo Durocher. BELOW: Toots sees his friend Corp. Barney Ross, USMC, a hero at Guadalcanal, receive award from Nat Fleischer of *Ring* magazine. Onlookers are former Mayor Jimmy Walker, former Postmaster General James A. Farley, and Murray Lewin, boxing editor of the New York *Mirror*.

White House bound—more or less. Toots, Frank Sinatra and Rags Ragland

ABOVE: Walter Walters, chief steward of Shor's, delivers a fifth of coal to Newcastle. BELOW: Celebrating Harry Truman's upset victory over Tom Dewey, November 2, 1948, at the Waldorf: (left to right) Mrs. Eddy Duchin, Mrs. Joseph Nunan, Peter Lind Hayes, Pat O'Brien, Toots and Baby, Mary Healy Hayes, Joseph Nunan, Eddy Duchin and Mrs. Pat O'Brien

ABOVE: Four pretty good country ballplayers, Frank Howard, Don Drysdale, Gil Hodges and Whitey Ford, drop by Toots's box, and nobody is prouder than Toots's son Rory. BELOW: Toots settling the ancient question as to which is more compelling, the pen (John Hersey) or the sword (Gen. Dwight D. Eisenhower)

CHAPTER 3

"...Put your arms around a millionaire."

TOOTS SHOR'S had tradition the night it opened. The nineteen years that followed at 51 West 51—until the iron ball swung against its ruddy brick walls in 1959— enriched the lore and legend. They were memorable times in the life of the city, the proprietor, and the customers who survived the rigors of knowing him well.

Toots bloomed and ballooned during those strenuous, exciting and exhausting years. He worked, bet, laughed, cried, and drank harder than probably anybody else in New York or, conceivably, the world. He virtually lived in his place except for brief time-outs to have dinner with Baby and the growing brood of handsome children at their impressive duplex at 480 Park Avenue. The only real vacations he took were from booze. Once a year he retreated to Hot Springs, Arkansas, there to dry out, take the baths and cut up old touches with Owney Madden, who had retired to that sanctuary, far from the madding crowd, and incredibly married the postmaster's daughter. The only other times Toots would be out of his store, as he called it, were during summer weekends. He took a liking to the Jersey shore and rented rambling old homes in Deal during the hot months. He paid five thousand dollars a season for one fine home year after year, refusing to buy the whole place, furnished, for twenty thousand. "Why pay twenty when I can get it for five every summer for the next ten or fifteen years?" he asked the bewildered real-estate man. Toots even joined the exclusive Hollywood Golf and Country Club at Deal before learning that few of its rich Jewish members dared to drink with him. He took up golf under the world's most patient club pro, Lou Barbara, and ignored critics like Jackie Gleason, who likened Toots's golfing style and skill to that of a cow playing ice hockey.

Back at the store, every day was Mardi Gras and every night New Year's Eve.

After a fight, for example, his bar would be smothered six-deep by sportswriters, managers, bucket-carriers, and fans —Hemingway was often there—all arguing about the justice or injustice of the decision in the main event, or the precise blow that dumped the loser. There was much gesturing and punch-mimicking that tended to spill drinks. Toots starred in most of the arguments. In a chitchat column Earl Wilson wrote: "Overheard at Toots Shor's—Toots Shor." In short, his bar was the place one had to go or risk the loud censure of the proprietor next time in. The recrimination could be heard on occasion through the whole restaurant. Once when Toots was away in Hot Springs, a minor poet at the relatively hushed bar wrote:

> The joint is qui-e-ter
> Without the proprietor.

Toots was not to be believed, at least by certain patrons who happened to drop in. A complete stranger from the Middle West wrote Toots:

DEAR MR. SHOR:

My wife and I dined at your restaurant one night during our recent trip to New York. We found the food excellent, the drinks very nice, the atmosphere and service fine. But if you expect to make a success in your business you'd better get rid of that fat slob of a head-waiter who spent most of his time insulting patrons.

There was never a dull night at 51 West 51. There could hardly have been, considering the cast of characters.

One night Toots and Gleason, whose combined weight totaled nearly six hundred pounds, became embroiled in an argument over who could run faster. Neither seemed aware of the unlikeliness of the subject matter. Upshot of the de-

bate was Toots's declaration that he would bet Gleason
fifty dollars he could run around the block faster. The rules
were quickly established: they would run in opposite di-
rections, to avoid pushing or tripping, and the first one back
to the bar would get the fifty. And off they went, Toots
toward Fifth Avenue, Gleason toward Sixth.

Toots gave it his all. Wet and winded he staggered back
into the place and beheld a stunning sight. Gleason was
standing nonchalantly at the bar, a half-finished drink in
his hand. Toots paid off. Five minutes later he suddenly
stopped in mid-sentence and his eyes narrowed.

"Hey, just a minute," he said, poking Gleason in the chest.
"How come we didn't pass each other?"

"Simple," Gleason said grandly. "I took a cab."

They were a lot funnier than *The Odd Couple*. Toots,
who is something of a nonlistener, was addressing himself
at great length to some grave world problem one day at
the bar and was somewhat steamed up over the fact that
his listeners kept laughing through his monologue. They
were laughing at Gleason, who was pretending to be hang-
ing on every word. Instead, Jackie was now and then saying in an almost inaudible tone: "Get a load of the fag tie
on Toots."

Gleason fell upon bad times during the early days of the
restaurant and Toots promptly and generously "gave him the
pencil." Within the Shor cult, that means tab-signing privi-
leges: eat, drink, and be merry, and pay whenever you get it.
Gleason was not bashful. He became the best-fed out-of-work
actor in the land, and he always finished off his Henry VIII
banqueting by signing on a large tip for the waiter. The
waiter, of course, would rush the bill to the till and get his
handsome tip in cash. Toot's patience with this largess finally
petered out, and he apologetically asked Jackie not to tip
so big with his (Toots's) money.

"And have your waiters call you a cheap bastard?" Gleason
demanded, shocked. Toots never mentioned it again.

Toots bested many a brave drinker who came clumping
into 51 West 51 demanding a bottle bout. Toots even engaged in back-to-back doubleheaders. One long night he

knocked out his friend Curly Harris. Curly remembers fainting and falling as he dipped into his second fifth of Scotch. Toots had actually polished off a fifth of brandy as a warm-up before beginning to contest Curly drink for drink. Now he had finished two bottles and was breezing into the third when his opponent threw in (or up) the towel. While still coherent, Harris kept gloating, "I'm killing you, Toots."

"The next thing I remember is that it's morning and I'm back at the Elysee Hotel," Curly said recently. "I ran into Paul Douglas; he's living there too. I said, 'Paul, I killed Toots last night. Knocked him out. He's out like a light.' Well, Paul had been measuring Toots for some time, thinking of challenging him, so he figured now was a good time. He dropped into Shor's after he finished work that night and challenged him. Toots was standing at the bar having a social drink with Rags Ragland. He told Douglas to wait a bit while he had a warm-up fifth. Then the drinking started.

"The next day's matinee was the only performance of *Born Yesterday* Douglas ever missed," Curly says.

But the bout that is still spoken of in awed tones usually reserved for reminiscences of Waterloo or Dempsey-Firpo is the epic that pitted Shor against Gleason.

They drank head to head from noon to about 6 P.M. At that point Gleason stood up for a stretch. He promptly fell with a resounding crash and lay there on his back, his ample body blocking the entrance to the dining room like a scuttled tanker immobilizing Suez. Waiters and captains leaped to his aid.

"Leave him there!" Toots roared. "He made his load, now let him get up himself." Jackie couldn't. Patrons arriving for an early dinner were forced to detour around one of the best-known stomachs in America, while Toots enjoyed the rest of his bottle.

Their routine exchanges would launch lesser men into mortal conflict.

"You've got the head of a pig," Toots once interrupted while Gleason was pursuing some point that bored Toots, or which he couldn't understand.

"And you've got the body of one," Gleason said, then went on with his point.

Watching Toots rolling up a flight of steps, Gleason observed, "Toots going upstairs looks like two small boys fighting under a blanket." He has never been heard to criticize Toots's bar, which Toots once called "my roulette wheel." But Gleason was never one to spare Toots's kitchen.

Once he sent out for a couple of wheel-sized pizzas and ate them with great flourish at one of Toots's more desirable tables. "Had to do it," he explained to curious passersby. "Can't stand the food here." One Friday night during the trying time when he was broke but eating and drinking well off Toots, Jackie borrowed ten dollars from the proprietor.

"I'm going next door to the Gloucester for dinner," he explained to Toots. "Great seafood."

Gleason came in for lunch one Wednesday and found all the tables filled and a line of suburban ladies waiting to be served before going to the matinees.

"Sorry, Jackie, I don't have a table for you right now," Toots said. "Why don't you go to the bar and I'll call you when I've got something." But it was Gleason who called.

"Hey, Toots," he said, loud enough for the ladies in waiting to hear. "You still serving those contaminated sand-dabs? You want to get in trouble with the Board of Health again? You *know* what they told you." The ladies drifted uneasily toward the exit. Checks were called for at several tables and the diners left. In a short time Gleason was able to move with style to an empty table, accompanied by Jack Lescoulie, Lee Meyers, Bullets Durgom, Ed Byron, and one or two others he had met at the bar and invited to be his guests.

Toots gave him a hard time through the afternoon until Gleason silenced him with a stern threat.

"Toots," he said with great dignity, "if you don't lay off me I'll turn in my pencil!"

Gleason and Toots have a lot in common: they are reformed pool hustlers. Listening one night to Gleason's long recitation of how great he was, Toots was struck by a happy thought. He went to a booth, made a quick phone call and returned to the table. Then he suggested that he and Jackie go to a neighboring poolroom and shoot a little. While there, Toots spotted a friend, greeted him warmly, and introduced him.

"Jackie, this is Arnold Schulman from Philadelphia," he said. "We been friends since we were traveling salesmen together." Then Toots carefully goaded Gleason into playing Schulman for money.

Gleason is a fine player, but that night he was completely demolished. At the end of his rout and after paying off, Gleason was reintroduced. Schulman turned out to be Toots's good friend Willie Mosconi, the world's champion.

Toots's triumph was deflated not long after that in another bet involving names. Phil Silvers and he were talking baseball one day at the beginning of the season. Silvers was a great fan of Ted Williams of the Boston Red Sox. Toots at that time was so close to Joe DiMaggio that they were sometimes mistaken for lopsided Siamese twins.

Silvers offhandedly said, "Williams is going to have a great season. He'll outhit DiMaggio fifty points, I'd say."

Toots began seething.

"You wouldn't want to bet on that, would you?"

"Sure," Phil said, all innocence.

"Thousand?"

"Make it five thousand," Phil said airily.

"You got a bet!" Toots boomed. They shook hands and Phil started for the door. He opened it and stood there.

"I just want to verify the bet, Toots," he said. "I've got Williams, right?"

"You know what you can do with him," Joe DiMaggio's number one champion said.

"And you've got *Vince* DiMaggio," Phil said, mentioning for the first time the name of Joe's brother, who had been setting imperishable records for being struck out ever since entering the National League. Phil escaped as Shor lunged for him.

From the start there was never any question as to who was boss at 51 West 51. Not even the neighborhood's freeloading cops dared to drop by for an off-duty drink or to mooch a meal after Toots ran the first such intruder off the premises and reported him to his honest lieutenant. He had no trouble with firemen either, even those who made a practice of barging into other places during a peak hour and plunging into the kitchen "to put out the fire." Unlike some other restaurant owners, Toots refused to pay them to stay out of his place. On opening night, Justin's four proud partners showed up for dinner and appeared to some old friends of Toots to be a bit overpossessive.

"Your new partners are taking over?" Grad Sears asked Toots bleakly.

Toots gave him a big smile.

"It's their night," Toots said.

They were the discreetest of partners. Most patrons thought Toots was sole owner.

For all his newfound power, Toots maintained a certain humility. The restaurant was embarked on its way to an annual gross of $2-million but Toots never became a "dude'y guy," his definition of someone who puffs up on his own importance and tends to address others with "How dee-ya-do?" His hide remained as impervious to the shafts of insults as that of a rhino. One night, sitting with Washington sportswriters Shirley Povich, Vincent X. Flaherty, Bob Addie, and another, Toots was loud in his praise of a column Bill Corum had in that evening's *Journal*.

"Who read it to you?" Shirley asked.

Toots rested his chin on his fist like Rodin's "Thinker." His face began to redden.

"That's a hell of a thing to ask," someone said to Shirley. "You've hurt Toots's feelings."

"No he didn't," Toots said, looking up quickly. "I was just trying to think who *did* read it to me."

He could be equally even-tempered in the face of impatient or complaining customers. Toots's motto reflected his abiding faith in his waiters: The customer is always wrong. Louis B. Mayer, a towering figure in Hollywood before whom thousands trembled or fawned, complained one night on leaving the restaurant that he and his party had been given bad service.

"I've seen some of your pictures," Toots said. It was in the great tradition of Ring Lardner's "'Shut up,' father explained." Charlie Chaplin, not known for his patience, once peevishly told Toots that he had been kept standing in line for a table much too long a time. "Let's see you be funny for the next twenty minutes," Toots said. Neither Mayer nor Chaplin ever came back. That was true, too, of the tough guy with a blonde on his arm who barked at Toots for keeping them waiting. He was losing face with the broad.

"I'm getting out of this place," he said, pushing his girl toward the revolving doors.

"No hooks up you," Toots said benevolently.

"And what's more," the tough shouted in a little curtain speech as the doors flipped by, "I'm going to tell all my friends to stay out of here!"

"Tell him," Toots said, just as the fellow committed himself to the doors.

Toots soon became as righteously proud of the patrons he had run out of the place as the dignitaries and celebrities who came in. One night he asked one of his best friends, sportscaster Ted Husing, to leave the place for saying "damn" and "hell" within earshot of a neighboring table of ladies. Deeply offended, Husing left in a huff. (Toots later was in large part responsible for getting up the money that paid for Ted's brain tumor operation and costly months of recuperation.) He felt no such sentiment toward Harry Wismer, another outstanding sports broadcaster of that period. Wismer, who had married into the Ford family, was in the throes of setting up a New York Ford agency to be owned equally by himself, Toots, and Horace Stoneham. But Toots and Wismer argued one night over some forgotten issue, the culmination of which was Wismer's threat to "get" Toots's liquor license. Toots not only barred Wismer "for life" but excoriated him with his worst curse. He called Harry a piece of raisin cake.

It has always been give-and-take with Toots. Late one night at the bar he objected to something said by one of his all-time ring idols, retired undefeated heavyweight champion Gene Tunney. He invited Tunney to "step outside." Tunney looked at him incredulously, then decided that the pavement in front of Toots's saloon was not a proper setting for a come-back. Particularly at those prices. (They became great friends.)

Toots could be patient too, and an uncomplaining host. In the early years of his first restaurant he would throw a grand party each Christmas night for friends and their wives who had suffered through a long and exhausting day with their children. Toots knew what kind of ordeal that was. So the mob would gather about ten o'clock in the evening, with assorted children all safely tucked in their beds, and make merry. Feature of each year's Christmas party, held on the second floor of the otherwise darkened restaurant, was a skit written and acted by Toots's theatrical friends. They always wrote in a part for Toots and he rehearsed his lines like a diligent schoolboy. But for years they never gave him the full script, and for years the final act of the play always saw Toots getting a meringue pie pushed in his face. It always came as a surprise, like Good Old Charlie Brown's disastrous opening-day pitch.

He was given a memorable surprise party on the occasion of his fiftieth birthday. Baby and their good friends Joe and Catherine Nunan, got Toots out of the store for dinner that night while the invited guest/hosts assembled in the second-floor dining room and the actors and other talent set the stage. Toots knew the room had been rented by Frank Fol-som of RCA but was led to believe that it was for a party for show people. As the evening with his wife and the Nunans wore on, Toots became restless. Baby insisted on going to El Morocco for one more drink, but Toots made one of his rare stands against her.

"Jiminy crickets," he wheezed. "I want to get back to the store, Husky, and say hello to Frank. Let's go."

The sight of a room packed with his friends, all standing and singing "Happy Birthday" as he entered, was almost too much for Toots. He left his wife and the Nunans and did a crazy running dance down the left-hand side of the room, listing heavily to port. Then he cried for a while, kissed every-body, and sat down for some heavier drinking and to see the show. It was something to see: Ethel Merman, Bert Wheeler,

Eddie Fisher, Pat Harrington, and many others. Gleason was M.C. For a big finale, Gleason called for a roll of drums and bawled, "And now, ladies and gentlemen, the surprise of the evening: Toots's first girl friend!"

Jackie went to the wings of the improvised stage and led out a goat.

For an encore, Rags Ragland hit Toots with a meringue pie. Lemon.

Toots always found friends easy to forgive, though he was a bit jarred during the height of one of the Arab-Israeli wars when he received a phone message at home from his head captain Joe Harrison, asking him to come to the store immediately.

"Hurry, Toots," Joe said. "Six Saudi Arabians just walked in for lunch, all in their robes and headpieces."

Toots hopped a cab. Only a few nights before he had made a hair-raising pledge to Edward R. Murrow. Ed had come in from a formal dinner involved with aid to Israel. He was more somber than usual. "Toots," he said after a few silent drinks, "when I die I want to buy it while fighting with the forces of Israel." For Toots, who had been at Temple that day, it was the most extraordinary pledge of aid since Lafayette's.

"I'll go witcha!" Toots said, bolstering his patriotism with another brandy-and-soda.

So it was with some heat that Toots entered his place and found the forbidding-looking gowned Arabs knocking over their third round of drinks. He was about to wade into them and order them out when he recognized one of them under his heavy tan makeup. It was a chronically out-of-work actor who used to hang around the joint.

Gleason had hired the lot of them, paid for their costumes, and sent them to Shor's.

But it was not all bread and circuses at 51 West 51.

In 1943, Toots was caught with his points down. The OPA (Office of Price Administration) announced that Shor was overdrawn by 103,000 points. Many of Shor's customers, reading the dismaying news from Washington, believed it to be a typographical error. They thought it might be pints, not points. But it was points, meaning, in effect, that the restaurant had purchased and served some 23,000 pounds more of rationed meat than it was entitled to at that pit of wartime austerity. The OPA verdict was that Shor could serve no meat until the overdraft was erased.

It took three months, and it produced some touching acts of loyalty on the part of his regulars. They risked scurvy at his place each day, confined as they were to poultry, fish, and eggs. Toots was never one to let sauces smother, disguise, or even complement his uncompromising dishes. Thus his drab fare at this period tended to stick to customers' plates while in the course of being consumed. One night two of his bravest loyalists, Mr. and Mrs. Jack Pearl, having had the fish at lunch, ordered the chicken. It was apparently Chicken à la Suction Cup. Spotting a friend across the room, the Pearls held their dishes up *vertically,* to show the friend what they were having. The chickens did not slip so much as a millimeter.

The crisis produced some memorable examples of Broadway journalese, as faithfully researched by the *New Yorker* magazine's John Bainbridge:

It's touching how Broadwayites have been flocking to Toots Shor's eatery to demonstrate their sentiments in the matter of his difficulty with the O.P.A.—which are that obviously Toots was a victim of his own honest intentions, and if the recent decision isn't reversed in his favor, there ain't no justice.—Dorothy Kilgallen.

Amazing is the loyalty exhibited by the hundreds of Shor's friends. This doesn't follow the usual picture of Broadway's callous indifference and fickleness.—Louis Sobol.

The Stem figures that big Toots, likable and decent, has been given a bum deal, so now his restaurant is minus meat, but not minus customers. Mrs. Toots, who is as tiny as her husband is huge, has been badly worried by the crisis through which their restaurant has been passing. The baby, Bari Ellen, 5 months, 14 days old, continues to coo and gurgle happily. She doesn't know that her Pop's been on the spot—Ed Sullivan.

Grad Sears wired from the West Coast, "I don't love meat. I love you." Jimmy Walker told friends, "Now we've got to eat at Toots's twice a day instead of once." The former mayor did too. On Fridays it would be a doubleheader of scrod.

Toots remained 110 percent patriotic in face of this harassment. Indeed, when a customer complained about the midnight curfew on New York bars, Toots uttered a patriotic line that has been put right up there with the fervored sayings of Patrick Henry and others. Looking sternly at the plaintiff, Toots said, "Any bum can't get drunk by twelve o'clock ain't trying."

The big war meant a lot to Toots. Some of his best friends were always going to it, calling him or writing him from far-off places, or coming home. Toots felt bound to see them off, try to send booze to them while they were there, and weep with joy over their return. Toots had an early ecumenical attitude toward military rank. One of his finest efforts was a kind of state dinner in honor of Pvt. Al Buck of the New York *Post*, a fine, pale, indoor type whose greatest previously known physical effort was to walk across the pavement to get into a cab bound for either Madison Square Garden or Shor's. Things being what they were, the Army assigned Al to the Rangers and sent him through a horrifying obstacle course that had him back at Shor's, in civvies, before Toots had thrown out the last bum at Al's farewell party. On the other side of the coin of rank, Toots was able to fly half a dozen bottles of Haig Pinch, six bottles of prewar bourbon, and a mound of Havana cigars to Saipan for Maj. Gen. Rosy O'Donnell, leader of the first B-29 raid on Tokyo.

Some of Toots's best friends began dying about that time and an entire new sideline opened for him. He had always been a sentimental slob about death, but now that he had the money to afford it he could pull out all the stops. Campbell's Funeral Parlor at 81st and Madison became Toots's "home away from home," as Frank Conniff put it. Certain rituals were shaped: the wake and many embraces of the bereaved, the funeral services (always too early for Toots and other mourners who had spent the better part of the night reminiscing about the late-lamented), and then the after-funeral fun. This latter always began on a fairly solemn note at the bar of the Stanhope Hotel at 81st and Fifth Avenue. It is a cheerless place that discourages drinking, but it is still the nearest saloon to Campbell's and one of the rare pubs whose bartenders must be rotated from some obscure bar in Bucharest. They never recognized Toots, despite his king-sized thirst and tips. So, for many years that place at the Stanhope has been but a stepping-stone to enable mourners to subdue their grief until they get farther downtown to Shor's—which opens early on funeral days. And stays open longer.

There is no truth to the legend that George Jessel once came up to Toots and said, "I've got some bad news for you, McKinley's dead," whereupon Toots burst into tears and ordered mourning drinks all around. But it should have happened. Toots would have played his role with great sincerity. Funerals stimulate him to such a degree that a close friend recently said to him, quite sincerely, "Toots, lemme know when it's convenient for you for me to die. Would you like it to be a weekend?"

When Leo Justin died, Toots closed his place immediately for the rest of the day and night (Justin's partners kept their theaters open because "Leo would have wanted it that way") and he was inconsolable for a week. There were times when even Baby didn't know where he was, except that wherever it was he was drinking and weeping. The day President Roosevelt died Toots angrily threw everybody out of his place, locked the doors and got drunk with the bartenders. Then he went to Temple and prayed for the repose of the soul of his hero—who had interrupted a campaign swing through New York City one raw day in 1944 to summon Toots from inside 51 West 51 and have a friendly chat with him at curbside.

He was to close his place the day of President Kennedy's assassination too. Even if he had wished to remain open, he could not have done so after the news flash from Dallas. "The help got loaded with me," Toots recalls.

Toots became so good at funerals that he found himself in charge of those of his more personal friends and relatives.

Two of the memorable ones were those of his beloved mother-in-law and Bill Corum. Mom Volk was a Catholic, Corum a Baptist. But Toots took care of everything with commendable efficiency and traces, here and there, of sentimentality and piety.

His patience ran somewhat thin, however, when an extraordinary number of distant relatives and even more distant friends of Mom Volk showed up at Campbell's to pay their last respects. Many of their last respects reduced the already grieving Baby to further tears. Some of the long-lost male relatives and friends of friends of Mom repaired immediately to Toots's bar and announced they would have one on the house. Toots searched through Campbell's for one of *his* friends and found him as the man—who happened to be a papal knight—entered, intent upon saying his Rosary at the side of Mom's bier. Plunging through a fortune in funeral wreaths and baskets, Toots embraced the mourner.

"Thank Christ you're here," he said, "those goddam Catholics are driving me nuts."

The Corum funeral, which forever deprived Toots of an irreplaceable friend and adviser, was later described by one of the mourners as "three days of solid laughs." It was not an irreverent statement. It was just a fact. The laughter was interspersed with certain solemnities, notably a moving reading from the Good Book by Episcopal layreader Red Barber, the sports broadcaster, at Campbell's. After touching base at the Stanhope, and being given a temperance stare by the bartender, the keeners were trundled to Toots's to commune with his more communicative bartenders and have a fast bite before going on to LaGuardia and the plane for St. Louis. Bill was to be interred in Boonville, not far from Speed, Missouri, where he was born and whose name he had done his best to emulate through life. Toots had bought out a large section of the plane. He paid for all the tickets of the funeral party, including Corum's.

Toots put everybody up at St. Louis' posh Chase-Plaza for the night and provided a handsome bar and dinner. The next morning he piled them into half a dozen rented Cadillacs to follow the hearse to Boonville. It was a long parched trip through at least one dry county, particularly for the late-lamented's good friend and consultant (on horses) Lee Meyers. As the entourage took off from St. Louis, Toots noticed that Arthur Mann, the serious-minded baseball historian who was helping Corum with a book when Bill died, was alone in one of the limousines. Toots ordered Lee to get out of the car in which he had settled down with Conniff and others to join Mann for the ride.

"There goes half our laughs," Conniff said as Lee reluctantly made the change.

Toots had forgotten that Mann hated racing and Lee loathed baseball. When at long last the cars reached Boonville's old and rickety hotel and debarked the generally happy mourners—the route had led through a wet county too—Meyers came back to the car in which he was originally to have traveled. He looked exhausted.

"Ask me something about Babe Ruth," he said to Conniff.

Toots took charge of seeing that the body reached the local funeral parlor and that Mom Corum, a remarkably spry woman of ninety, and Bill's passive brother Clayton, got to the place to meet the Missouri mourners. Then, before setting out for Columbia to take part in a TV tribute to the man who was a product of the Missouri University School of Journalism, Toots gave Meyers an order. "I'll be back in an hour or so. In the meantime you case Boonville and find the best bar and restaurant."

Two hours later when Lee led Toots's little group there, Toots glared at the garishly lighted lunchroom.

"You call this the best joint in Boonville?" he demanded. "It looks like a toilet in Penn Station."

"You should see the other joints," Lee said, and then added unhappily that it served nothing hard to drink.

It was almost too much for Toots, but he sat down and was determined to make the best of things. There was some consolation: Mom Corum was comfortable at the funeral parlor, Clayton was sober, and a lot of their old friends had come to be with them. There was a further consolation. One of Toots's friends at the table had taken the precaution to bring along a three-bottle Mark Cross leather liquor case designed for just such expeditions through dry lands. He had filled one of the bottles with brandy—for Toots; one with dry martinis —for Conniff; and the third with Scotch—for himself.

A slatternly young waitress hovered over the table at the start of things, ready to pour coffee. Toots had never had a drink of coffee in his life. He clapped a righteous hand over his empty cup, and while the girl's attention was drawn to other cups Toots beckoned for the surreptitious brandy. His cup was quickly filled. He was just about to take a gulp— it had been a hard day—when the waitress wheeled, nostrils twitching.

"That's whiskey!" she shrieked. "Don't you dare take a drink of that in our restaurant or I'll call the police." She said much the same to the owner of the provisions, who was pouring himself a Scotch, and cowed him too. In the meantime Conniff had poured a huge clear martini into his water glass.

"May I have some ice in my water?" he asked sweetly, with the dimples no girl in her right senses could resist.

"Certainly, sir," the waitress said, attending to same. "Now what would you like for dinner, sir?"

"It's Friday," Frank said. "I think I'll have some nice fish. What kind do you have?"

"We got one order of catfish left," she said. She raced off and brought it back immediately. It had been fried in Essolube at some incalculable earlier date. A denizen from some deep Missouri mud flat, it had whiskers like a walrus. Frank dug in with relish, after toasting Toots with his martini.

"Boonville's a great seafood town," Frank said, chomping away.

"Disgusting," Toots said with a shudder.

Toots was called to the phone before he could order. He was wanted at the funeral parlor. He was back in half an hour, white-faced and shaken.

"Mom's had a heart attack," he said. "I got her to the hospital." Then he added, glumly, "Looks like a doubleheader tomorrow."

If it had been a doubleheader, some of the mourners from New York would have had trouble lasting through it. Horace Stoneham and his associate Garry Schumacher, long-time friends of Bill, had rolled in late from San Francisco. Horace poked a fifty-dollar bill in the hand of the elderly Negro porter—the hotel's only bellhop—and nobody thereafter could do wrong. It was a good, long, wet night and early morning, particularly after Stan Musial of the St. Louis Cardinals and effervescent Jimmy Conzelman arrived. Inmates of the hotel and families in neighboring houses learned much that night from Schumacher, who was in especially good voice. Garry's voice can carry over great distances without aid of electronic devices. This night the windows were open in his room, which helped. He and Bill had worked for years on the New York *Journal* and each was as knowledgeable of war strategy as they were of, say, baseball or football. Bill had been the youngest major in the A.E.F. Garry was an informal but astute authority on Napoleon. On this night of mourning he, or someone in the room, recalled a memorable debate he had once had with Bill on the military greatness of the emperor.

"If he was so wonderful, how come he blew the big one at Waterloo?" Bill asked, feeling he had sent in a crusher.

Garry coughed for a time, spraying ashes from the cigarette he always carried on the side of his mouth.

"Bad bench," he said in a magnificent defense of his hero.

Toots was awakened shortly after daybreak by Mom Corum's doctor. He was upset. Mom Corum had just announced to him that she was going to attend her son's funeral, and she wanted her clothes. Toots had to arbitrate. Solomon would have been proud of him. He struck a life-or-death compromise: he'd take the responsibility of having Mom leave the hospital and go to the church but he would not let her climb the twenty-odd steps that led up from the pavement to the church door. He would provide a chair in which she could be lifted up the steps by two of the abler bodied mourners from New York.

At the church, however, Mom Corum refused the chair.

"I'll walk to my boy's funeral, not be carried," she said with great dignity and resolve. And she did.

The funeral oration was brief, and unusual. It was the first homily ever given in the First Baptist Church of Boonville,

Missouri, by a Knight of Malta, who narrowly avoided falling into the total immersion tank.

Mom Corum went the distance, over the protests of her doctor. She journeyed to the graveyard for the grueling final rites. She held up superbly, much more so than the deceased's wobbly friends.

"Would you and your friends like a drink?" a delightful lady who was a friend of the Corum family whispered to Toots as the funeral party took sad leave of Bill's last resting place.

"Would we like a drink?" Toots said, much too loud. "Sadie O'Grady, would we like a drink!"

So the limousines, no longer led by a hearse, fell in line briskly behind the car of Boonville's beautiful benefactor. There was a bit of shoving and elbowing at the door of her home, especially when Toots and Herman Hickman tried to enter at the same time. Herman was as heavy as Toots but he had the height to carry it: five-feet-six.

Then a stunning discovery. The drink the lady had in mind was coffee. Pots of it, plus good things prepared and brought in by the neighbors.

"Try some of this delicious potato salad," a kindly woman said to Toots, the most ashen of the visitors.

Toots declined weakly. He explained that he never ate on an empty stomach.

But relief was in sight. The group was raced to a neighboring airport. Toots had chartered an Ozarks Airlines DC-3. Moreover, since many of the mourners were on the stout side, he had ordered that the armrests be stowed. Everybody had a double seat to himself. And in each seat Toots had provided a bottle of exactly the brand of booze that particular person liked. He had even found a bottle of Jack Daniel for Hickman, and a fifth of Old Rarity Scotch for the Pope's friend.

Even before that stellar performance, Toots had become the high priest, or rabbi, of his regular customers. Except for occasional rages he was a kind of East Coast distributor of benevolence. Men who could buy and sell him a hundred times over sought his advice, even on fiscal matters. Each year Ben Fairless of United States Steel held a princely party on Toots's second floor for fellow tycoons who headed the nation's largest corporations, and Toots would be the only outsider invited to break caviar with them. He was equally attentive, however, to the down-and-out among his friends, passé actors and athletes, extinguished stars, newspaper stiffs looking for a better opening. He ran an informal employment service with mixed success. Once he solemnly assured Bill Hearst, Jr. that a newsman who had drunk himself out of a previous job with the Hearst organization had become the greatest temperance leader since Andrew Volstead. Hearst was impressed. He agreed to rehire him. But the next day when Hearst entered the restaurant for lunch the first thing he saw was the reporter, stoned in a phone booth. Toots had better success with Frank Sinatra. Frank's appeal had been receding since his screaming little girl fans had reached the age of reason. Toots called Bob Hope and asked him to give Sinatra a break on his next TV special. Sinatra recouped all of his lost fame with a singularly brilliant performance, went on from there to play Maggio in *From Here to Eternity*, and has been an all but unparalleled star ever since.

(With some of his first newfound money, Sinatra bought expensive watches for Toots and their good mutual friend Rags Ragland, who was then down on his luck. Ragland's watch was engraved "From Riches to Rags.")

Toots developed a strong proprietory attitude toward "my guys." There was no way to shore up Shor's affection for them and sometimes overpowering interest in them. If any of them developed a toothache Toots had just the doctor for them. When Babe Ruth was dying of cancer, Toots divined that the best and most nourishing food for him would be great portions of fresh lobster bisque, which he dispatched to Babe's hospital room each night. Toots didn't like the modest reception plan the Professional Golfers' Association concocted for the arrival in New York of Ben Hogan, his friend, after Ben won a British Open. So Toots called up Mayor Vincent Impelliteri and ordered a ticker-tape parade for Ben. Earlier he had good-naturedly threatened to flatten Joe Louis if the heavyweight champion, who was shy about such matters, further balked at dining at the restaurant.

One day a manufacturer stopped Joe DiMaggio on the street and said, "Joe, why did you turn down my fifty-thousand-dollar offer to endorse my product?"

DiMaggio was stunned.

"I never heard of it," Joe said.

Now the manufacturer was stunned.

"I talked to Toots about it and he said you wouldn't be interested," the man said.

Joe headed for Shor's, as much of a compulsion in those days as heading for home.

"Yeah, I turned the creep down in your name, Dago," Toots said. "He isn't our kind of bum."

Toots protected his celebrities assiduously. He would growl and the growl would chase any patron of the restaurant, young or old, who tried to interrupt a celebrity for an autograph, no matter how willing or even eager the luminary might be. Any person who entered 51 West 51 with a camera and attempted to use it would be sternly lectured or thrown out. He would not give the time of day to any gassy stranger who hovered over the table where he was eating, drinking, or just talking to one of his guys. Corum was a particular plague to Toots at times like this. Unerringly cordial, Bill would say to the fumbling or even offensive stranger, "Won't you sit down and have a drink with us?" One night Toots got up and left his restaurant rather than sit with some fellow Corum had invited to join them. Hours later, making the rounds, Corum ran into Toots at Ed Wynn's Harwyn Club. He had hardly dropped into a chair beside Toots to have a drink when a stew from the bar came over and burbled, "Hi'ya, Bill, remember we met once at a Columbia-Yale game before the war?"

"Of course," Bill said warmly. "Won't you sit down and have a drink with us?" That drove Toots back to his own joint.

Toots loved Bill through thick and thin. When both needed the money, they could do remarkable things with checks written and cashed before 3 P.M. of a Friday, with nothing to worry about until 9 A.M. Monday, except where to spend the money. Toots often worried about Bill's health, a habit Toots has never been able to break. One day when he entered his place for the lunch period, Toots found Bill at the bar drinking a martini. Toots frowns heavily on the martini as an institution. He calls them "bombs," and confines most of his own limited consumption of them to his airplane trips—on which he knows the Federal regulations will restrict him to two.

To Toots's mounting dismay, Corum had several more martinis before lunch, a couple during lunch, and a few more during the afternoon and evening. As dinner approached he added a few more. After dinner, Toots asked him what he'd like in the way of a cordial or something.

"I'll have a martini," Bill said to the waiter.

Toots exploded.

"Jiminy crickets, Bill, you shouldn't drink the same drink all the time," he said. "You should mix them up, change over to something else after you've eaten."

That made good sense to Bill. So he ordered a Gibson.

The finest men's dinner given at 51 West 51 during its nearly two decades of gourmandizing was in Bill's honor. It commemorated his being elected president of Churchill Downs and (during his two-month leave of absence from his column) chief entrepreneur of his favorite horse race, the Kentucky Derby. (The previous year, his final one as a reporter of the event, Corum had astonishingly picked the order of finish 1-2-3-4.) Government, business, and sports figures from all over the country were in attendance at the Corum banquet. Toots personally arranged the seating and with a clear eye to dinner companions' interests, likes, dislikes. Each guest at the black-tie affair was outfitted with a blue ambassadorial type sash. Don Ameche, who had blown a fortune on the horses, was an irreproachable master of ceremonies. The entertainment would have bankrupted the Waldorf-Astoria: Ethel Merman, Frank Sinatra, Jimmy Durante, and Eddy Duchin. Great pools of beluga caviar rested in concaved backs of graceful swans of ice. The dinner bore little resemblance to the fundamentalist grub being served to the paying customers downstairs. (Toots never believed in putting anything on his menu that he couldn't pronounce.) The wine was Dom Pérignon, bountifully poured under curious orders from the host. "Don't hide that name with no dude'y towel," Toots had ruled.

On the way to Corum's first Derby as its majordomo, Toots announced one of his more memorable sacrifices in the name of friendship, his favorite word.

"You want to hear something?" he said to his seatmate on the plane. "I'm gonna drink only bourbon through this whole trip."

"Bourbon?" the friend said, lifting an eyebrow. "You don't drink bourbon. It makes you sick."

"I know," Toots said bravely. "But Bill's part of Kentucky now and I think I owe it to him to drink bourbon when I'm around him."

Which he did. Corum drank Scotch. And now and then martinis and Gibsons.

Toots remembers that Derby quite clearly, despite the bourbon. His daughter Bari Ellen made her First Communion that day in New York.

"Husky gave me a little hard time for blowing the Communion," Toots explained to friends. "But Bill needed me at the Derby." The customary hundred thousand also attended the race.

During the World War II years Toots was so busy running the restaurant and taking care of his multitude of friends, whether they wanted to be taken care of or not, that his gambling suffered. This was also partly because he had had a remarkable confrontation with the first and last of the true baseball czars, Judge Kenesaw Mountain Landis. It happened at the 1943 World Series which the Yankees won from the St. Louis Cardinals.

"Toots, are you betting?" the irascible old judge asked, brushing aside Toots's pleasantries. He meant on baseball.

"No, sir," Toots answered honestly. "Not since 1942." He spoke of that date as if it paralleled the Johnstown Flood.

"Good!" the judge snapped, poking a stilettolike finger into Toots's flabby chest. "Don't!" Toots swore eternal abstinence.

Toots had lost twenty thousand dollars on the Yankees in the 1942 Series.

"Moore killed DiMag," he cryptically recalls. That translates into something like "Terry Moore, the brilliant center fielder of the St. Louis Cardinals, robbed Joe DiMaggio, Toots's friend, of a long string of doubles and triples by a series of brilliant catches."

He kept his pledge to Judge Landis and renewed it with the judge's bland successors: Albert B. "Happy" Chandler (who deeply and doubly wounded Toots by barring Corum from participating in World Series broadcasts and by patronizing Billingsley's Stork Club); Ford Frick, Lt. Gen. William D. "Spike" Eckert, and Bowie Kuhn, the incumbent.

But as the big war ended and money poured into Toots's place by the bales, the old urge to get some action out of it once more overpowered Toots. Being able to afford to lose took some of the thrill out of his postwar gambling. But Toots soon found a way to blow enough to make him hurt. He discovered Billy Conn, the handsome, flashy light heavyweight from Pittsburgh. Billy had been discovered before the war, of course, when he won his title and then came dramatically close to outpointing Joe Louis for the heavyweight crown. Promoter Mike Jacobs planned a return match but Conn hurt himself in training and the blowup of Pearl Harbor put both men in uniform for the next four years.

Conn was mustered out right into Toots's lap. He lived at the Shors' duplex during his visits to New York. Toots became his adviser in all fields ranging from fiscal to the occasional fist fight Billy would have with his rough-and-ready father-in-law. Toots's keen knowledge of boxing kept nagging him: Louis was bigger, stronger, could hit much harder and was, in short, clearly the superior fighter. But naked knowledge never meant much to Toots when he was under the influence of hero worship. Billy would win, Billy would win, he told himself as he bet and bet and then bet some more. Billy agreed with Toots's estimate. Sure he'd win, sure he'd win. And to Toots's deep satisfaction,

Conn showed his genuine class. He went into hock to bet on himself.

Louis knocked out his pallid, listless, almost indifferent opponent in eight rounds without drawing a deep breath.

Toots is still guarded about how much the fight cost him in addition to the stacks of high-priced tickets he bought for friends and the long feeding and watering of Billy Conn.

"Six figures," he'll say, holding up six fingers.

"You mean $100,000 or $999,999?" a friend asks him occasionally.

"Six figures."

That was not Toots's only setback of the period. His good friend Matt Tracy and Tracy's brother Bob visited the Shors at Deal one weekend and decided to put in a day at the races at Monmouth Park. For Bob, the day began when he borrowed five hundred dollars from Toots. For Matty, it began with a question: "You want to be my partner?" Toots said yes, inadvertently setting in motion a somewhat harrowing sequence of events.

Bob returned from the track alone, early, and with the rueful news that he had blown the five hundred dollars. Matty came in later, just in time for dinner. They had gone through a few drinks and were well along with the meal when Toots could stand it no longer.

"Why don't you say something?" he demanded of his partner. Matty had not even mentioned what had happened to him at the track.

"Oh, I forgot," Matty said, reaching in his pocket. He pulled out his program and tossed it across the table to Toots. At the bottom of the last race he had written "plus $6,000." He explained casually that he had scored big on a horse named Lighthouse, after Bob had left the track broke.

"I had to go back to work Monday," Toots remembers, "but Matt was going to stay over, so when I left for New York, I told him I'd be his partner while he was down at the house. After all, we were fifty-fifty and so I was three grand ahead.

"Well, Monmouth closed in a few days and I didn't hear

anything from him except that he had gone to Saratoga. Then one day Bill Corum called from there to say hello and said, in passing, 'By the way I saw Matty lose twenty G's in a crap game last night.'

"I got Matty on the phone and told him, 'Listen, whatayadoing? I'm not in on any games like that. I'm only in on horses.' Matty said, 'Tootsie, you're in on every thing I do. I'm paying a hundred a day for a room up here; you've got half of it. Every time I buy champagne for twenty-five, you've got half of it. Every time I give a girl money, you've got half of it. Everything I do, you've got half of it.'" And he hung up on me.

"Now I begin hearing a lot of stories about how he won thousands here, thousands there. I'd call Saratoga and he wouldn't even answer the calls. I was going nuts. Then one day he called me. He was in Camac's Baths in Philadelphia. Seems he had left Saratoga and now was playing the horses at Garden State. Matty said, 'I've got eighty G's in my kick and I'm coming into New York. Get me a room.' Get him a room? I felt like buying him one. I got him a room at the Warwick so he'd be handy to the store when he came in with my forty—which I needed so bad. No question about it, I told some of the guys Matty was the best handicapper in the country; really knew the horses. And what he didn't know, a couple of top experts in Boston would tell him.

"Well, he didn't show up at the Warwick for a couple of days. He called me when he checked in and I asked him how we were doing. 'I got eighty-four hundred,' he said. 'We didn't do so good the last couple of days. But don't worry; we'll get well again. I got two good horses today. I'm betting two thousand on each of them to win.'

"They both got nosed out, and they were good long shots. So we split the forty-four hundred. I gave Baby my bit and told her to go buy something.

"Day or so later, everybody's celebrating at the bar when I came in for lunch. Seems that Matty had bet on a horse named North Pole II and it had paid a hundred and six dollars. So he looked over at me and said, 'Well, you fat so-and-so, I guess you're sorry you broke the partnership.'

"I didn't feel so good. After a time I said, 'Say, Matt, I want to ask you something. Who'd you get that horse from?' It wasn't the kind of horse his Boston pals would tout. And he said, 'From a rubber at the Pennsylvania Baths.'

"That's how my money was going."

The whopping losses put no crimp in Toots's plans for the property at 51 West 51. In 1946 he negotiated a new twenty-one-year lease that extended his control over the property until 1967 instead of 1961, the first termination date.

"I did it on my own," he says, pleased. "Shows you can do better without lawyers. If I hadn't made that new lease I never would have been able to make the deal I got eventually.

"I had about three or four hundred thousand in the bank at the time. I put my plans together: add a third floor, an office, new kitchens, so forth, and figured the three or four hundred thousand would easily cover it."

He was as optimistic on that as he had been on Conn.

"The job cost all the three or four hundred thousand and I wound up owing as much again by the time it was done," Toots says, shaking his head. "Imagine, the original joint cost one hundred and forty-one thousand—but now this enlarged joint cost seven hundred thousand. That meant more work for me, and harder meeting things. If Justin had been alive, I don't think I'd have had any troubles then or since.

"I had been getting kind of offers for the place for quite some time. One of the first offers was from Leonard Beck, who was the agent for the Astor estate. About 1942, Noyes wanted to sell me the property for about two hundred and some odd thousand. My accountant told me it wasn't worth buying because my rent was so cheap. So I didn't buy it. It's not important to own a property as long as you've got a long lease, right?

"So then Noyes called me again one day and I went to see him. He had gotten an offer of a million bucks for the property and I'm offered five hundred G's for my lease. Noyes said, 'Toots, why don't you take it?' I looked at him and said, 'Listen, I got a lease. This is mine. I built this place; you didn't build it. I put my money in there. *My money's* in there, not yours. I've got close to a million dollars in there. You didn't do it; I did it. Why should I sell cheap?' So I wouldn't do it.

"Finally, one day, it was the month of July, 1954, maybe 1955. I remember my daughter Kerry was sick. July was a tough month; things were rough. I owed a couple hundred thousand at the time, to dealers and people. So I said, well, I'll go over and sell the place for five hundred thousand, keep maybe three hundred thousand and go West with Kerry and the family. Maybe Phoenix or that part of the country would do her good.

"So I left Kerry's room at the hospital at nine o'clock one morning and walked over to Leonard Beck's office, ready to sell. He wasn't in. At twelve o'clock noon he wasn't in. During the afternoon I got a little bit morbid. Maybe it was loaded, not morbid. So I said, 'Aw, why should I sell now?'

"Then, I'll never forget, it's St. Patrick's Day a year or two later, and I'm standing there with Joe Nunan at the bar when guess who comes in? Leonard Beck. He wants to see me upstairs.

"He offered me a *million dollars* and put a hundred-thousand-dollar-check down in front of me. I could taste it. I needed about twenty G's in the bank that day. But I said no. He blew.

"I went back downstairs and told Nunan. Joe said, 'You might be the dumbest Jew in the world, but I can't say you don't have the most guts I ever saw.'

"So I go along for a time and then John Galbreath, the big-shot real-estate guy, came to me. How'dee'y' do, Tooots. Like that. He wanted the property. He offered me three floors in the office building he was wanting to build in that block. But that flopped. Then he said he'd buy the Berkshire Hotel, enlarge the Barberry Room to three floors, pay for the alterations, and give me a million bucks—all that, if I'd sell him 51 West 51."

Toots, for all of his suspicion of lawyers, had retained one by that time: Arnold Grant, well-known in New York legal circles.

"Arnold made a contract with Galbreath that had a clause in it saying that if Galbreath didn't finish the three-story restaurant in the hotel by such and such a date, he'd have to pay me a certain amount more. I showed the contract to Jock Whitney. [Toots had endeared himself to Whitney earlier by sending him a ten-dollar money order for his birthday.] Jock said, 'Who's that lawyer you got? *I* want him.'

"Now something went daffy. I don't know what it was. Now they want to build me the joint in the Berkshire, okay, but give me five hundred thousand, not a million, and promise me seven percent on the five. Galbreath said, 'You know, To-o-o-ots, we're in baseball together.' He had the Pirates. '*We* don't need a lawyer.' I said, 'John, when it comes over half a million dollars, *I* need a lawyer.' So the deal fell through.

"Now Bill Zeckendorf comes in, wanting to take over the property rights. He offers me a million. Grant's still my lawyer so he goes to work on Zeckendorf. Zeckendorf offers me a million-three. I said no.

"The restaurant was doing pretty good but I still owe a couple hundred thousand, maybe more, on the enlargement. And I've got to think of my partners. They'd put up fifty at the start. I had given them back over two hundred, but they're still my partners.

"Finally Grant called me up one day—I'll never forget, it was the month of August, 1958—and he said Zeckendorf wanted a sixty-day option on the place and he'd pay me a million and a half. I checked it through with some people and they all said it was a big price. So I told him to make the deal.

"So now on September eighth—no ninth—I'm sitting with Mickey Mantle and Whitey Ford, having a long lunch. I dropped them off at the St. Moritz; they were going to get a plane to Cleveland. I went home and about six I got a call from Zeckendorf. He said, 'Toooots, can you come down to ...' oh, someplace around Wall Street. I said I didn't know how to get there, so he said, 'I'll have a car pick you up at nine o'clock.'

"So I go down to the Chase Manhattan Bank—I don't remember the name of the street. We sat around down there until about two in the morning. Zeckendorf is clowning. Finally they all signed the papers and the checks. There were two of them. One was for a million-one, I think, and the other was for four hundred thousand. They were going to take off four or five thousand dollars for a few things I owed, like the water bill. I said, 'Gentlemen, will you please give me the full amount—a million and a half. I want to show it to my wife.' So they handed me the checks and I handed them my personal check for the five thousand.

"I looked at their checks and said, 'I hope these are good, because if they aren't, well, the one you're holding is no good either.' "

Toots drove uptown with one of Zeckendorf's lawyers. He let him off at the Commodore then took the limousine on to 480 Park. His place was closed. It was three thirty and all was still in the apartment.

Toots groped his way through the darkened bedroom and gently woke his wife.

"Husky," he said, "put your arms around a millionaire."

CHAPTER 4

"...Thousands of bums will be homeless."

"TOOTS was COD in ninety days," Zeckendorf said recently. "He's very much like me, I'm sorry to say. He's improvident."

There is a difference between the two improvidents, however. On Toots, improvidence is becoming. He and his friends had a whale of a time spending his fortune. All hands agreed that Toots, normally difficult to bear, would be impossible as a millionaire.

Getting rid of $1.5-million got off to a disappointingly slow start. Toots, having broken the dazzling news to Baby, walked over to Rubens to have a drink and maybe run into some late drinkers he knew. He half succeeded.

"I sat at the bar and had an American B. and B. You know, brandy with a beer chaser. I was just sitting there thinking and having a few when some guy down the other end of the bar yells at me, 'You don't know anybody anymore, do you? I knew you when you were a bum on Forty-ninth and Broadway.'

"I looked down at this fellow and started to steam. But then I said to myself, 'What am I doing getting into a fight with this bum with a million and a half in my kick?' So I took another drink, paid the check, and walked home, the richest bum in town."

Happily, the velocity picked up as soon as Toots arrived at his joint around noon. He called for his often harried accountant, Dick Sherman, and handed him the two checks. Dick scanned them quickly and the blood went out of his face. He appeared to be about to faint.

"Toots, you know what these checks come to?" he asked weakly.

"Deposit them," Toots said. And then with a gesture which might have confounded J. P. Morgan, Toots added, "Put the dough in my checking account."

If anything, Dick went even whiter.

"But Toots," he said, "the bank doesn't pay interest on checking accounts. I'll put it in a savings account and they'll start paying you three or four percent, right off. It'll amount to thousands . . ."

"I said put it in my checking account," Toots repeated, his voice rising. "I'll show those creeps at Irving Trust!"

Often during the years before the day Toots became an instant millionaire he had engaged in a running war with that distinguished New York banking house. Each outbreak was caused by the bank's hapless habit of informing him whenever he was overdrawn and suggesting that he balance his account immediately. Now Toots would have his revenge. He'd prevent Irving from paying him interest!

With that happy thought in mind, Toots moved to the bar to announce the great news and buy everybody a drink. The word spread like wild flowers, as Sam Goldwyn once cogently remarked. Some came to congratulate him, others simply to drink with him, and still others to put the arm on him.

But one came intending to ask him if he was some kind of a nut:

"It was one of the vice-presidents from Irving Trust. One of those stiff-collar creeps. He gave me that 'how-dee y'dooo' bit. I said, 'Listen. You've never been in my saloon before now. Well, I want to tell you something: I'm the same guy today as I was yesterday. Now get out!'"

"But I only wanted to advise you that . . ."

"Out!" Toots boomed, turned back to the bar and ordered another drink all around.

It was one of the proudest hours of Toots's life, to be able to tell off a banker. He had chosen bankers in general as his natural foes many years before he came into his fortune. They angered him instinctively. They just didn't understand money. Money was printed to spend and give, not harbor. Toots felt it was his duty in life to show them the light by any means at his command. The readiest means was invective.

Horace Stoneham, eager to sell his hotel property in Sanford, Florida, once invited several of the city's better-known bankers to a rented suite in the Plaza. They accepted the bid, and Horace was so pleased he unwittingly invited Toots too. All went well for some time. Horace seemed on the brink of victory, and nobody in the suite was happier than Toots, aglow over his friend's impending affluence.

Just at that moment the top banker present turned casually to Toots, held out his half-empty highball glass and said, "Put some ice in my drink." It was an order, not a request.

"Put your finger in it and stir it, you creep," Toots said like jagged lightning. "You're a banker; that'll cool your drink."

For unexplained reasons, Stoneham didn't make his deal.

Toots and bankers in general were philosophically at odds in other details. The matter of using other people's money, for one. No banker could have understood a transaction between Toots and Bill Farnsworth, fabled sports editor of the New York *Journal*. Farnsworth dropped by Leon and Eddie's one afternoon when Toots was on duty.

"Let me have five hundred, Toots, I've got to go to Miami," he said, looking impatiently at his watch.

Toots was busted at the time. "I don't have it, Bill; I'm sorry."

Farnsworth was surprised. "You've got it in the till, Toots," he said.

"That's Leon and Eddie's."

"So what?" Farnsworth said with a shrug. "If I were in your spot and *you* needed it, I'd give it to you."

That made eminently good sense to Toots. He rang up 'No Sale', dipped in, and Farnsworth was on his way.

(Years later, when he wasn't doing too well, Toots turned down an offer which he now figures cost him millions. He was approached one day by a couple of well-dressed tough

guys who then controlled the newly opened Riviera in Las
Vegas. They made him an unprecedented offer. They would
give him ten "points," 10 percent off the top of everything—
the hotel and the casino—if he agreed to manage the spa.
Toots told them he'd have to think it over. This provoked
one of the men to say, "Do you want to leave your wife and
kids money or a reputation?"

Toots reached a strong fat hand into the fellow's collar
and pulled him up against his chest. "Don't ever mention my
wife and kids," he said, and threw both of them out.

"Jiminy crickets," he sometimes sighs. "Then Howard
Hughes comes along and makes everything in Las Vegas
as clean as a church.)

The day the $1.5 came turned out to be the kind of
day Toots likes best: friends around him drinking and reminiscing and his switchboard aglow with incoming and outgoing long-distance calls. His roastbeef hash was famous by
that time. But on that day the principal item on the menu
was rehash. Most sentences began with "Remember. . . ."

There was so much to remember, varied as a day in May
but singularly a part of the strange legend and folklore of
Toots.

Remember . . . the night after a New York Baseball Writers dinner when the only sober sportswriter at Toots's annual
postdinner, closed-door party was Lawton Carver, sports
editor of International News Service? Some bum had
crashed Toots's relatively exclusive portal. He offended almost everybody in the happy room. Toots was drinking and
didn't recognize offense, for a change. But Carver did.
Coming on strong with his sobriety, Lawton grabbed the
souse by the scruff of his collar and the seat of his pants
and propelled him toward the revolving door at great speed.
Alas, the door was locked. The drunk stopped on a dime as
he hit the door. Lawton hit the back of the bum's head,
flush on, and loosened a couple of teeth. He went out another door, looking for a dentist. The bum went back to
the party.

Remember . . . the night Toots put a knock on Dr. Billy
Graham and quick retribution was provided by his Irish-

Catholic Baby? Toots had heard that Dr. Graham, who was then leading his first New York Crusade, owned twenty Italian silk tailored suits. Toots took off on the great Protestant preacher at some length, most sentences beginning, "How about that Billy Graham coming into this decent town waving that Bible and saying he's going to save us, and him with all those suits?" Little Baby, delicate chin cupped in hand as she listened to the long harangue, turned to the others at the table and said, "Get a load of Bishop Sheeny."

Remember ... the late, late night when Ella Logan, star of *Finian's Rainbow,* came in with a memorable slapstick comic named Frank Libuse? The bar was sparsely attended, chiefly by proper couples who had missed the last train to Larchmont. Logan and Libuse had the whole act well planned. They took their places on adjoining barstools. Frank kept his hard straw hat on. "How vulgar," a Westchester matron sniffed. Frank excused himself and hung the hat on Ella's left breast. (She had equipped that side of her dress with a protruding fishhook.) Frank's drink arrived, and as the bartender served it to him Frank pulled it toward himself. It emptied in his lap. Frank fell off his stool with a resounding crash. When waiters tried to pick him up, the great clown tripped up the waiters and in time there was a great tangle of bodies on the floor. Ella indignantly walked into the neighboring door marked Ladies. Frank untangled himself from the fallen waiters and walked in right after her, to the gasps of the suburban couples. They stared, shocked, at the closed door. Then it opened just a bit and Frank stuck his bald head out. "Two beers!" he shouted to the bartender.

Remember ... the night Jack Kearns, who once owned 50 percent of Jack Dempsey, came in the joint after one of his latter-day woebegone fighters had won the duke at the Garden and borrowed a C-note from Toots and then tossed it on the bar to buy drinks for all the boxing writers on hand? Toots, with no chance of getting the hundred back, was deeply impressed by Kearns' gesture. "What class!" he said.

Remember . . . when those dirty crums hung a sentence
on Joe Nunan and put the former U.S. Internal Revenue
Service chief away for nonpayment of a lousy eight grand
or something? Toots had prayed mightily in Joe's behalf
as the Feds closed in. He would pray each day at St. Patrick's Cathedral, Temple Emanu-El, and St. Thomas', the
Protestant citadel on Fifth Avenue. When a friend asked
him why, Toots said grimly, "I'm touching all bases." When
the ax fell, Nicky Blair said to Toots, "You're a killer. You
drank Mark Hellinger into his grave, along with nine other
friends. You think Considine likes to go off to wars and
do all that traveling? He don't. He's just trying to escape
from you. Look at what Joe Nunan did to get away from
you!"

Remember . . . the night Quent Reynolds talked Toots
into making up with Sherman Billingsley? Quent's case was
presented so well that Toots put on his hat and coat and
left his place, headed for the Stork Club. It promised to
be the greatest peace treaty since that of John Wayne and
Geronimo. Ten yards down the street, Toots stopped. He
said to Quent, "If you needed three hundred, who would
you go to?" Reynolds thought for a moment, then said,
"You." They turned and walked back into Shor's.

Remember . . . the way Bob Hope told him that he had
found a way to spring Frank Sinatra from his contractural
and other troubles and get him a spot in television? "I'll
never forget," Toots said then and now. "It was May sixth
at Louisville. I went out to the airport to meet Bob and
Dolores. He said, 'Don't worry about Bones. He's on my
next show.' What a thrill that was. It was also Bari Ellen's
birthday."

Remember . . . the night Horace Stoneham and his friend
Dick Flanagan got in an argument at the bar and invited
each other outside to fight? Neither could, especially at
that time of night, but out they went. Toots witnessed the
challenge and the departure but remained at the bar. He
had seen and participated in too many of those confronta-
tions. But after a time, when they hadn't returned with their
arms around each other, Toots became worried. He was

worried mostly because he suddenly remembered it was raining hard. He went outside and stood under the awning. Neither challenger was immediately in sight.

The gladiators were half a block away. They were circling each other slowly and unsteadily, each using an ancient Jem Mace pose. Not a punch had been thrown. Toots's proper doorman was holding his umbrella over them.

Remember ... when Leo Justin died and Toots went on his freak-out and spent most of his time at Moore's? Toots did.

"Moore was a tough, old-time saloonkeeper. He used to put salt on the edge of his glasses and throw a lot of salt in his stews to make people thirstier and drink more beer. He was daffy, like all of us. I'll never forget, one day Rags Ragland and I were standing at Moore's bar having a drink when the old man came over and growled, 'C'mon, stop drinking. Have some coffee.'

"Rags said, 'Coffee killed my old man.' I looked at him and asked him what he said. 'A three-hundred-pound bag of it fell on his head,' Rags said.

Remember ... one Sunday night when Toots's three most trusted men—Jack Barry, Bob Broderick, and Joe Harrison —went to a late spot for a nightcap after Toots's had closed?

Well, at 4 A.M. the bartender asked the three to leave or else he'd blow his license. They did reluctantly, wishing there was some other place to go.

"I know a spot," Broderick suddenly remembered. "The Bismarck."

"Where's it at?" Harrison asked.

"Chicago," Broderick said. "It's open all night."

"So let's go," Barry said.

They groped their way to LaGuardia Airport and caught the first plane out. About six o'clock the next night, with their wives calling Toots anxiously and Toots about to send out a police search for the bodies, he received a telegram. It read: "Dear Toots. See you Wednesday. Keep smiling. Jack, Bob, and Joe." Several hours later they sent a wire to one of Toots's bartenders, asking for three hundred dollars. He scraped it together and wired it to them in Chicago.

That elicited another wire from the trio to Toots, saying that they wouldn't be back until Thursday.

They made it. When Toots came in at noon they were all there in their positions, freshly scrubbed, shaved, and in black tie.

Shor walked right past them without speaking. He maintained his austere silence until rather late that night. Then Barry grabbed him and said "For Christ's sake, say something to me, will you?"

Toots spoke. He was white with indignation.

"Why the hell didn't you take me with you?" he shouted.

Remember . . . what Seymour Weiss had meant to him all through the years? Toots could never forget.

"I first met Seymour when I had the Tavern. I don't know of any man who's done more for me in my life. He's the most wonderful, generous friend any man could have.

"Once I learned that our friend Joe E. Lewis was gambling too much. He was stuck for over two hundred G's in Vegas. I called Seymour at his Hotel Roosevelt in New Orleans and said, 'See what you can do to straighten Joe E. out. He won't listen to me because he figures I'm another bum like himself.'

"So Seymour flew all the way out there to talk to Joe E. and then he came to New York and gave me a report.

" 'Joe E. thinks he's you when he's drinking,' Seymour said, 'so I warned him about that.' I said, 'Seymour, I wasn't talking about his drinking when I called you. It's his *gambling*. What did you say to him about *that?*'

"Seymour said, 'Oh, I told him that as long as I had a hotel, not to worry.' "

Remember . . . Jessel's advice to Toots in regard to Weiss? He said to Toots, "Why don't you rehearse acting like Seymour one hour a day?" Toots had replied, resignedly, "How could a bum like me be a perfect Southern gentleman? That's what Seymour is."

Remember . . . the big night in Philadelphia when Toots got some sort of local-boy-makes-good award? Toots was so anxious that his best friends be present for the great occasion that he chartered a bus, stocked it with soft food and hard drink, and off it chugged to what by that time had become the most important event in Philadelphia's history since the arrival there of Benjamin Franklin. Toots had asked a dozen or so of his writer pals, "Write me a little something to say, please." They labored for days and coached him on how to pronounce all the big words. But when Toots stood up to respond to the award, the pages of his script began to rattle as if in high wind. Everything went blank. He put it aside, looked down at the floor like an abashed boy, and made his own speech. It had to do with his most sacred theme: friendship. The pained writers got stoned on the bus back to New York.

Remember . . . the suit against Billingsley?

Nobody remembered that one better than Toots. It took some telling. It had been one of the high points of his life.

The fateful day it all began saw Toots awaken in his grubby but expensive suite in Louisville's Hotel Kentucky. It was Sunday morning, the day after the 1955 Derby, and Toots felt good even though he had demolished scores of Hardboot Country drinkers and sportswriter friends the night before at the big party Bill Corum threw in his nine-room suite atop the grandstand at Churchill Downs.

He rounded up his entourage, Baby, Ameche, Arcaro, Conniff, and others, and got everyone aboard an Eastern Airlines Constellation in the nick of time. En route, Toots found an opportunity to defame Southern cooking. He patted the stewardess on her bottom and asked in his disarming way, "What's for lunch, honey?"

The girl thought for a time, puzzled, though she had already served thirty luncheons.

"I don't really know," she said, "but it *looks* like ham."

"Probably Southern-cooked," Toots announced to any in his part of the plane who cared to listen. "Name me something worse than Southern cooking. How can anybody eat that stuff?"

A Southern lady seated directly behind him took icy issue.

"Southern cooking is the finest cooking in this here country," she said with the fire of Scarlet O'Hara. "What would you know about cooking, anyway? I've eaten in your place."

Toots was stung, particularly when his whole group laughed out loud. But it was only a flesh wound.

"I still say it's the worst," he said to the lady. "Even canned goods taste bad in the South."

A Carey Cadillac was waiting at LaGuardia to whisk the Shor party to 480 Park and a continuation of the festivities which had begun the previous Friday when Toots and his friends arrived in Louisville and were taken directly from the airport to the track in cars provided by Corum.

The post-Derby party was still sounding loud and clear at 9:15 P.M. when "The Stork Club Show" came on even louder and certainly clearer on WABC-TV. It was a show Toots eagerly looked forward to each Sunday. It gave him an opportunity to call its star, Sherman Billingsley, all the things he wished he had said to him twenty-five years before, when Billingsley was firing him regularly from the mob-controlled speakeasies. "That bum needs an idiot card to say 'Hello,'" Toots said, pleased by the customary sight of his old foe fumbling all over the screen.

But then came that portion of the forty-five-minute show devoted to Billingsley's showing to one of his guests photographs of celebrities who had recently patronized the Stork. This fateful night the guest was Carl Brisson, the actor. He and Billingsley examined one photograph after another (they were shown full-screen as the men lavished praise on the personalities concerned) until they came to a picture that particularly arrested Brisson's interest.

"You know this fellow?" Billingsley asked.

"Ah, Toots Shor!" Brisson exclaimed. "Good looking but a little too much here." He made a curving gesture around his stomach.

"I don't think so," Billingsley said grittily. "I wish I had the money he owes around this town."

The stillness of Appomattox settled over the usually boisterous Shor apartment.

"Does he owe you any?" Brisson continued on the screen. He was a friend of Toots. (He came into Toots's place early the next day, near tears, to assure his friend that he had no prior knowledge of the cruel trick.)

Billingsley's reply to the question Brisson asked on the air was "No." The show went on to other matters, but the impression was left that Toots was in hock to everybody from Van Cleef & Arpels to the gents' room attendant.

The Shor apartment was suddenly rent asunder by a bellow of rage, followed by sniffles and tears from Baby.

"Out of my way!" Toots roared, coming out from behind the bar. "I'm going down there and invite that creepy, slimy, filthy, cripple-nosed piece of raisin cake to step outside."

"No you're not, Big Man," Ameche said, bounding off his barstool and grabbing him. But Toots dragged him and several others forward like a goal-plunging fullback as he headed for his hat. They couldn't stop him, but the telephone did. It was Conniff, by now at home.

"Don't do anything foolish," Frank told him, inserting his advice between Toots's rages. "Play it cool. You've got an open-and-shut slander case." Immediately after Conniff hung up, the phone rang again. It was Johnny Broderick. "I saw it and heard it," the retired but still bruising detective said. "I'm up in the country but I'm leaving right now and driving in to see that you don't do anything crazy."

There was no Shor-Billingsley fight that night.

Toots sued Billingsley for $1.1 million.

Months of legalistic dickering followed, further aggravated by crowded court calendars. Billingsley made several unsuccessful efforts to effect an armistice, using emissaries who were as welcome at the Stork as they were at Shor's. One was Corum, who rather abruptly ended Billingsley's appeal to him to serve as an arbiter.

"I just don't understand it, Bill," Billingsley said as they sat at a table one night in the Stork. "What's Toots got that I haven't?"

Corum thought a bit before he spoke.

"Sherm," Bill said, "the difference is that Toots has got class."

Toots was comforted through the long wait for the court action to begin by the tone of the mail he received. People who had never been in his place wrote him, offering to serve as witnesses to the slander.

Mrs. Aaron C. Goldman, of Hazleton, Pennsylvania, wrote:

> It was with a great deal of pleasure that I read in the paper recently of your pending suit against Mr. Billingsley. Though not given to letter-writing in affairs not concerning me, I couldn't resist the chance to congratulate you—and hope that you are successful.
>
> My husband and I have long bemoaned the fact that the powers that be on television are so undiscriminating in their choice of programs. Billingsley, to us, epitomizes all that is tactless, obnoxious, and in bad taste. The night he said what he said concerning you, we first cringed, and then one of us said, "I hope he's sued!"
>
> Why do we watch? Because we have long hoped that Mr. Billingsley would overstep his bounds, and we wanted to be around to see it!

Philip Van Doren Stern, the author and editor, came forth with:

> DEAR TOOTS SHOR:
>
> I have often eaten in your restaurant, but you do not know me. I am writing to you because of an article I saw in the *Herald Tribune* about your suit against Sherman Billingsley.
>
> In 1938 a similar thing happened to me and my attorney was able to collect damages from the National Broadcasting Company for every station from Maine to California that carried the program. Since NBC settled readily out of court, they evidently thought I had so valid a case that they wanted to squelch it. If my experience is of any interest to you or to your attorney, I will be glad to give you any information I have on the case.

There was a pretrial hearing in Arnold Grant's office, after many delays.

"Hello, Toots, how are you?" Billingsley said with a radiant smile as he entered the room with his lawyers. Toots growled. When the questioning later came around to the pictures that had been shown on the offending TV show, and who had selected them, Billingsley named this and that selector on his staff. Asked to identify the person who had included Shor's picture—a profile view showing him against the Stork's bar with two somewhat sinister-looking characters—Billingsley grinned and acknowledged, "I'm afraid that *I* picked that one." It had been snapped in 1939.

Arnold Grant lined up the notable former New York Supreme Court Justice Simon Rifkind to represent Shor in court. There were additional delays, however, during one of which Shor and Billingsley met by accident late one night in the spring of 1957 at Rubens' bar. Billingsley, at one end of the bar, was accompanied by two detectives. They were on a search. He had demanded the arrest of a young Stork Club employee he accused of making a pass at his, Billingsley's, secretary. Spotting Toots at the other end of the bar, Billingsley shouted a foul epithet. Toots started for his old foe, who was always armed. But once more Ameche, this time with the help of John Ringling North, pushed him back. Billingsley and the detectives left the place.

The next day one of the detectives dropped by Shor's to apologize and Toots read him out.

"You should've locked him up for using dirty words in public," he lectured the plainclothesman. "Now, I could call your captain right now—he knows me better than he knows you—and have him bust you for standing by and doing nothing in a case like that. Billingsley would, if you had been standing next to me and I did the cursing."

Billingsley soon did just that. One day while the suit was still pending he noticed that a group of painters, working on a house next to his, were using the steps to the Billingsley home for their lunchtime break. He pulled out his gun and the men fled. One fled to the nearest cop.

That evening one of the most respected inspectors on the force phoned Billingsley at the Stork and said he was sorry but he had to pick him up for booking on the gun charge. The inspector said he didn't wish to cause any commotion at the Stork and asked Billingsley to meet him at the corner of 53d and Madison, a block away. They met and walked together to the nearest precinct where he was booked and quickly released on bail. Billingsley promptly set about the task of trying to discredit the discreet inspector. He charged that the man had accepted from him a puppy and other presents the previous Christmas. The inspector was finally given a clean bill of health by his superiors, but only after a searching inquiry. It was the only complaint that had ever been made against him.

On the night of the booking, Billingsley returned to his place and did something rare. He took a drink or two. A couple of reporters who had ready access to both the Stork and Shor's dropped by the place and found him sitting alone, fathoms deep in silent anger. They sat down with him and ordered a drink. Billingsley ordered a glassful of the Stork's drink-stirrers, eight-inch blue glass sticks. He chose one from the glass and began toying with it. Then he began talking in quiet but increasingly angry tones about Shor.

Suddenly he jammed the glass stirrer into the tablecloth like a dagger. Glass splinters flew this way and that. Over the next half hour he smashed all the stirrers as he developed the foggy thesis that Shor was the cause of all his troubles, including his long-running feud with the waiters' union. The table was littered with broken glass when the reporters, who had been shielding their eyes with every blow, made good their escape to the nearest bar for a tranquilizing drink.

The case never came up. Billingsley settled for fifty thousand dollars.

"Rifkind could've taken half of it as his fee," Toots remembers. "But he took only ten grand. Real classy guy." Grant had served Toots gratis.

Toots did an extraordinary thing with the forty thousand dollars, which was tax free. He put it in an untouchable trust for his children's education.

"I know the Man up there liked that," he told a friend.

Toots meant God, the only close friend he has who doesn't eat in the joint.

The day of remembrance was a long one for the city's newest millionaire. The night was longer. At the end of it, Toots slid slowly downhill from mellow to melancholy. Unable to bear the thought that he was now richer than most of his best pals put together, he called for his checkbook and began writing ten-thousand-dollar checks. These he stuffed into the nearest breast pockets around him. To their credit, the checks the old pals received were returned the next day. One was so startled to find Toots's ten grand in his pocket the next morning, during a routine frisk of his suit before sending it to be pressed, that he hired a Carey to return it to Toots at his apartment. Counting the tip, it cost him twenty-five dollars to return the ten grand.

By now Toots was as big a sport as the Big Town had ever had, and that included a legendary fellow millionaire of similar girth, Diamond Jim Brady.

But good friends continued to resist his largess. He called Matt Tracy in Palm Beach and offered him $100,000 to set up his own horse book. He laid down one condition: Tracy must not do any gambling himself. There was a long pause on the line from Palm Beach.

Then Matt said, "No thanks, Tootsie."

Toots rates that rejection high on his list of displays of class. Right up there with the turndown he got from Tony Canzoneri. The former lightweight champion had not been doing well with his small saloon off Eighth Avenue in the Fifties. Toots dropped in for a drink at the place, the Paddock, a day or two after the big score.

"You all right?" he asked Tony after a shot or two.

"I'm okay, Right Hand," Tony said. It was his name for Toots. Barney Ross also called him that.

"I've got ten in my kick if you need it," Toots said quietly.

The tough little man who had made a fortune with his fists shook his head, and set up another drink for Toots.

"He died a week later in his room, alone and broke," Toots says. It always moves him near to tears.

So does the memory of a time when he was having fiscal miseries and Barney Ross dropped by the store, took Toots aside and whispered, "I've got eight for you."

"The last eight of his life, I've always figured," Toots says, sadly.

Also near the top in Toots's book of classy performances is the name of Ken Venturi, winner of the 1964 National Open at the Congressional Country Club, near Washington. Seems that Venturi was so lowly regarded he was not among the pros invited to attend the pre-tournament luncheon at the White House.

Venturi won the title in 100 degrees of heat and 100 of humidity. He suffered so badly from heat exhaustion that his doctor insisted on walking at his side through the final crushing day—at that time a 36-hole test of endurance. On the first green of the last eighteen, Ken's long putt stopped on the lip of the cup. It was so frustrating to see it becalmed there that he thought of taking his doctor's advice and giving up.

But then the ball dropped in for a birdie—so if that was the kind of day it was going to be, he'd go as far as he could stand up. He was barely moving as he came up the long final hole. His gallery by that time had swelled from his doctor and his wife to thousands of fans cheering his gameness. There was an explosive ovation when he putted out for the championship.

Among the millions who watched the ending on TV was President Johnson. He had an aide call Ken and invite him to the White House for dinner.

"I can't make it," Ken said over the locker-room phone. "I've got a dinner date in New York with Toots Shor."

The joint gave him a standing ovation when he walked in.

With all his well-publicized moves and statements it was inevitable that television would insist that Toots face the boob-tube.

In videoland, as elsewhere, he was unique. Even before he became an instant millionaire.

There were many debates over which was the worst television show of the 1950's. Several responsible critics went to their graves convinced it was a Ralph Edwards' "This Is Your Life" starring Toots Shor.

The show is best explained by the inch-high lettering of the TelePrompTer script, a large bale of bathos which Toots somehow treasures right up there with such tributes as Joe E. Lewis' during the period when Toots was caught with his meat-ration points down. Joe, who was commanding his top salary at Ciro's in Beverly Hills, told an interviewer: "I'd rather be standing outside Toots's starving than sitting inside Ciro's belching."

The producers of "This Is Your Life" went to pains to enlist the services of Quentin Reynolds as Toots's personal Pied Piper on that night of nights. And vice versa. The plot was that Quent would invite Toots to the Colonial Theater to watch an early demonstration of color TV. Toots was then informed separately that Quent had been suckered into the promise to attend; that the producers were going to spring a big surprise on him and call him before the cameras. Quent, the ploy went, would therefore need the comfort of knowing that Toots was in the audience. (The concocters of the intrigue are believed to have later headed up the Bay of Pigs invasion plans.)

After a highly forgettable exchange between the commercial announcer and "America's Most Beautiful Reporter," Jinx Falkenberg—in which she revealed she had been using Hazel Somebody's lipstick for two long years—Edwards intoned via TelePrompTer:

BUT NOW, ON WITH THE SHOW! . . . TONIGHT WE'RE GOING TO PULL A DOUBLE SWITCH. . . . YOU'RE ABOUT TO SEE TWO MEN, ONE OF WHOM THINKS HE IS FOOLING THE OTHER IN A LITTLE AD LIB TELEVISION TEST. . . . ONE IS THE WORLD-FAMOUS CORRESPONDENT AND AUTHOR, QUENTIN REYNOLDS. . . . THE OTHER, NEW YORK'S BEST-KNOWN RESTAURATEUR, TOOTS SHOR. . . . THEY'RE COMING THROUGH THE STAGE DOOR RIGHT NOW . . . SO

I'LL DUCK BEHIND THE ARCHWAY. . . . TAKE IT AWAY, CAMERA NUMBER ONE!

TOOTS—It's sure great isn't it, Quent, to be here in the world's largest color television theater.

QUENT—Yes, but what's even more exciting to me is that while this is being telecast in color the millions of viewers across the country will also be able to see it in black and white, eventually.

TOOTS—Quentin, I've got news for you. They are seeing it right now not only in color but also black and white. We've played a big trick on you . . . this is no fifteen-minute interview about color television. We're on coast to coast right now.

QUENT—Wait a minute, Toots. . . . I've known all about that right from the start . . . you thought I didn't know about "This Is Your Life" and all that business. Well, I know more about it than you do because this isn't my life, Toots Shor. This is *your* life!

(Applause. Music.)

RALPH—Hello, Toots. Your good friend, Quentin Reynolds, is right. For a smart Broadway character you never thought this could happen to you. Did you, Toots?

(Answer.) *

RALPH—This is probably the most elaborate hoax we've ever perpetrated on "This Is Your Life." We know that it would have to be just that to fool you. Thank you, Quentin Reynolds for your wonderful help . . . you have a place in Toots's life later on, you know. So take a spot in his past for the time being. Come over here, Toots. Sit here in our chair of honor and surprises . . . and what a procession of surprises are in store for you. "This Is Your Life," Toots Shor.

(Music.)

RALPH—From a childhood spent in middle-class obscurity, through many ups and downs, you, Toots Shor, have risen to the eminent position as owner of one of the world's great restaurants . . . gathering place of the great and near great. You've done this through your ability and desire to make and hold friends.

---

* Toots answered with something that sounded like "Gulp," then cried through the next half hour.

(*Music.*) *

RALPH—You were born in South Philadelphia, weren't you, Toots? Indeed you were ... on May 6, 1903. ... Your father and mother were Abraham and Fanny Shor. ... They owned a little cigar and candy store, over which they had their home. What is your real name, Toots?

(*Answer.*)

TOOTS—Bernard.

(*Offstage voice.*)

VOICE—I have a picture of Bernard that shows how he got the name of Toots.

RALPH—Whose voice was that? Do you know?

(*Prob. will recognize.*)

RALPH—Yes, your sister ... for over thirty years now a government employee in the Philadelphia Navy Yard ... Miss Esther Shor. And here she is!

(*She enters. Music.*)

RALPH—Now, what about this picture you have, Esther?

ESTHER—Here ... see ... weren't you cute, Toots?

(*Reaction.*)

RALPH—Look at those curls!

ESTHER—Our darling aunt called him "Tootsie" ... stuck to him ... when he got too big it became just "Toots."

RALPH—Now, we know that your brother has an almost unlimited capacity for friendship. Did this show up in his childhood?

ESTHER—He has hundreds of friends ... he's generous to a fault ... as a boy, whenever we had fishcakes he gave them away.

RALPH—A trait that since then has often made him poor in material possessions but always rich with the love of his friends. Thank you, Miss Esther Shor!

(*Applause. Music.*)

RALPH—You had a happy childhood, didn't you, Toots? Rolling marbles on the Philadelphia sidewalks and playing baseball on the street in front of the family candy store ...

---

* Laced with choking sounds from regular patrons who were in the audience or out there in videoland.

sometimes the cops would chase you off, wouldn't they? What did you kids use to do then?

(*Go to store . . . mother. Bat . . . hold off cop.*)

RALPH—Your mother was a great companion and inspiration to you, wasn't she?

(*Answer.*)

. . . until her tragic death in an automobile accident in 1918 when you, Toots, were just fifteen . . . you were a good student up to this time, but with your mother gone, you began to skip school and neglect your studies . . .

(*Offstage voice.*)

VOICE—He ran away to Atlantic City a couple of times. But mostly we bummed around the corner of Broad and Federal and played pool at Joe's Poolroom, or at Coward's.

RALPH—Now, there's someone who knows a lot about you, Toots. Who is it? Do you know?

(*May not.*)

RALPH—He was a constant companion of yours from the time you were fourteen and until you reached twenty . . . you haven't seen him for thirteen years . . . so here he is . . . from Philadelphia, Lou Baldino!

(*Applause. Music.*)

RALPH—Was Toots here a good pool player in those days?

BALDINO—Everybody said, "Look at that kid . . . sometimes he make as much as six dollars a day."

RALPH—Where did you learn to shoot pool, Toots?

(*Church . . . YMCA.*)

RALPH—You never got into any real trouble, did you, Lou?

BALDINO—No . . . just some scrapes . . . Toots once hit a fellow with a cue . . . but it wasn't serious.

RALPH—Well, boys will be boys, I guess.

(*Laughter.*)

RALPH—What do you do now, Lou?

BALDINO—I'm a magistrate in the suburbs of Philadelphia.

A long commercial in which Jinx had a good word to say for Hazel's Complexion Glow and the Edwards show ("I love 'This Is Your Life.' I laugh and cry every week I watch it,"), gave Toots a much needed opportunity to stop crying and prepare himself for the emotional rigors to come.

RALPH—What was your first job here in New York?
(*Bouncer.*)
RALPH—I'll bet you were a good one, Toots!
(*Offstage voice.*)
VOICE—He sure was, Ralph. That's why we hired him as an inside doorman at our place.
RALPH—I'm sure you recognize that voice, Toots.
(*He does.*)
RALPH—Another friend of many years . . . one half of Leon and Eddie's, formerly a famous New York nightspot . . . here he is from Melrose Park in Fort Lauderdale, Florida . . . Eddie Davis!
(*Music. Greeting.*)
RALPH—Leon and Eddie's was a pretty popular place here in the early thirties, wasn't it, Eddie?
EDDIE—It was tops . . . Toots's friendliness helped make it even more popular.
RALPH—Lots of celebrities going in and out of the place . . .
EDDIE—Yes . . . Jolson . . . Crosby . . . everybody of any consequence.
RALPH—It was here, too, that Toots first started dreaming of someday owning a restaurant of his own, right?
EDDIE—I guess so. He asked a lot of questions and we didn't have to explain things to him more than once.*
RALPH—But six years of hard work . . . of hope and despair . . . were to elapse before your dreams of a Toots Shor restaurant were to come true . . . but first, let's think of 1934 . . . November 2. No date in your life, Toots, is more important than that one, is it? Yes, that's the day you and the lovely Irish chorus girl, in Jack Benny's Broadway show *Bring On the Girls* . . . Marian Volk, were married. And here she is to share this night with you, your wife, Baby!

Baby handled the cloying questions about their married life with skill. Meanwhile, the TelePrompTer was unwinding relentlessly:

---

* Eddie appeared nervous as Toots embraced him on screen. He said later that he had become quite deaf and had rigged his hearing aid with a double brace of batteries for the show. "I was afraid Toots would cry on me and electrocute me," he explained.

(*Offstage voice.*)

VOICE—There probably isn't a ballplayer in the major leagues who isn't a friend of Toots . . . but his heart has always been with the New York Giants.

RALPH—Surely you know who that is, Toots. Yes, your dear friend of many years . . . the manager of the team you are always rooting for . . . Leo Durocher!

(*Music. Applause. Greeting.*)

RALPH—Toots is quite a Giant fan, eh Leo?

DUROCHER—One of the greatest . . . he loves all sports . . . knows as much as any manager, coach, or sportswriter.

RALPH—What's the longest baseball game ever played in the majors, Toots?

TOOTS—A one-to-one tie between the Brooklyn Dodgers and the Boston Braves back in 1920. It went twenty-six innings. Called on account of darkness.

RALPH—The boy really knows his stuff, doesn't he, Leo?

DUROCHER—What did I tell you? . . . He's a rabid fan. When the Giants had a seven-game losing streak not long ago Toots said, "I wonder if I'm a good father, raising my kids to be Giant fans. I wonder if I'm doing the right thing by 'em?"

RALPH—Whether they grow up to be Giant, Yankee, or Dodger fans, he's doing the right thing by the kids all right. Do you happen to have Bari Ellen's report card on you, Toots?

(*May have.*)
(*Offstage voice.*)

VOICE—Toots Shor is a nice man.

RALPH—No one needs to be told whose voice that is.

(*Sure don't.*)

RALPH—Yes, one of the great comedians of our time . . . star of Broadway and television . . . Jackie Gleason.

(*Applause. Gleason greeting. Ad lib.*)

RALPH—Thank you, Jackie Gleason.

There followed a moist-eyed exchange with Pat O'Brien, and proud embraces of Bari Ellen, then ten, Kerry, seven, and Rory, three, all introduced by loud thumpings from the band. Then Ralph's solemn invocation:

TO THE PRESENT THE STORY IS NOW COMPLETE, TOOTS SHOR ... RESTAURATEUR TO THE WORLD ... FRIEND OF THE FRIEND-LESS AND FRIEND OF THE FAMOUS. WE SALUTE YOUR PAST, YOUR PRESENT, AND YOUR FUTURE.

Jinx came back with a touching story about how she had to do her nails every day, being a typewriting reporter, but then she discovered Hazel's nail polish. Hazel's polish, Jinx said, stayed on beautifully for a week. There were other kiss-blowings at the polish.

Toots went back to his store and polished off a fifth of brandy, awaiting the reviews of his smashing debut in show biz.

Toots gave television another chance, and vice versa, the following season. An odd little man from St. Louis named Teddy Nadler had become the marvel of the then still credible quiz-show craze. He swept through CBS's "$64,000 Question" and then moved on to the network's "$64,000 Challenge." CBS brass was eager to get rid of him and find a more personable performer. The perfect opening came when Nadler, who apparently had not attended half a dozen major league games in his life, chose baseball as the subject on which he would challenge any contestant CBS selected.

CBS rolled out the barrel: Toots. He was the undisputed chief archivist of baseball facts and figures not worth remembering. He accepted Nadler's challenge for two reasons: (1) he condemned all alleged sports authorities who preferred to watch their favorite games on TV instead of buying tickets and showing up in person and, (2) he just happened to need $64,000.

Unlike Randolph Churchill, another stout and stouthearted celebrity who foundered on the first question: "Who was Captain Boycott?" Toots matched the incredible Nadler week after week, while millions cheered. On each big-show night he would shave, shower, and climb into his Sunday best and take a limousine to the studio accompanied by Baby, his adoring daughter Bari Ellen, and good friend Frank Slocum

of Commissioner Ford Frick's office. Nadler would walk over
from his broom closet in the McAlpin Hotel, having spent a
stimulating afternoon memorizing the baseball record books.
Champion and challenger would enter their "isolation booths"
to shattering musical salutes and God only remembers what
goo from Hal March. Came the fatal night when Toots was
going for $32,000—halfway home!

"Most of the people on that program were straining for a
house or a yacht, but Toots was there to get even financially
and socially," Slocum remembers. "He not only needed the
sixty-four grand but he wanted to put Nadler down. It was
a grudge match. Toots had decided that Nadler had given
Bari Ellen the brush when they were introduced. So by the
time he's going for the thirty-two, it's a vendetta. At least it is
in Toots's mind."

Toots blew the $32,000 question. It was "Name five of the
seven men Don Larsen struck out in the perfect game he
pitched in the World Series against the Brooklyn Dodgers."
Toots instantly named three and then began to sweat. The
toothy host of the show noisily implored Toots to guess.

"I could stand here and guess," Toots said. "Sports guys
don't guess. If we don't know, we don't know."

"If he had guessed he'd have had a good shot at the thirty-
two grand," Slocum says. "There were only ten Dodgers used
in that game. He would surely have remembered Sal Maglie,
who pitched against Larsen, would have been one of those
Don fanned. The price was with Toots. He had bet so much
before that, on occasions when the price wasn't right. But
he bowed out. Nadler rattled off five of the seven guys who
struck out as if they were his roommates. He had probably
never seen any of them in real life. Toots knew them all.

"Baby took it real good but Bari Ellen was really shook,"
Slocum recalls. "We went back to the store and got a real
bad break. Paul Douglas came in and sat at the next table.
He had played Harry Brock, the rich junk dealer, in *Born
Yesterday*. A lot of people thought the character had been
shaped after Toots. But that night I knew it wasn't. Douglas
had seen Toots blow the dough but when he started to needle
our table he didn't needle Toots, who could take it. He

needled Bari Ellen, who had been close to tears for half an hour. Toots was furious.

"Whatever Paul's strong points were as an actor, he *was* Harry Brock."

In time, Toots found a silver lining in his defeat at the hands (or memory) of Nadler: "Yogi Berra didn't know the names, and he caught Larsen that day. Phil Rizzuto, Larsen's shortstop, didn't know. And guess who else? Larsen!"

As the last days and nights of 51 West 51 came and went with regrettable speed, Toots was troubled by more than the vast waves of sentimentality that immersed him. Zeckendorf was undergoing one of the dips in his roller coaster fiscal life. His dream of building a vast new hotel to fill half a solid block between 51st and 52d, facing Sixth Avenue, and naming it the Zeckendorf, had gone glimmering. So had the two million dollars he invested in plans for the massive pleasure dome. By that time abler financiers had gained control of Zeckendorf's leases and decided to erect the present Sperry Rand Building. Zeckendorf almost transplanted his hotel hopes to the area now occupied by the New York Hilton, but he missed again. At the time his deal with Toots had been signed he was on one of his financial peaks. He verbally assured Toots that he, Zeckendorf, would find him a good site for the new Toots Shor's and see that it was ready for him in a jiffy. But now Toots was the least of his troubles. He liked Toots but his mind was filled with bigger crises than where or whether a fellow could build a new saloon.

The new holders of the lease on 51 West 51 were even less concerned. They wanted to get started clearing the ground and digging the foundation for their skyscraper. Toots could feel their hot breaths on his neck throughout the speech he made at a nostalgic dinner in his honor, tendered him by his 250 closest friends. Toots's theme, as far as could be traced, was friendship.

Charles Champlin caught the spirit of the wake for *Life* magazine:

From cocktails on the second floor ("There wasn't a dry throat in the place," said one pal) the party moved to the third-floor dining room. "Sit down, ya bums," Toots suggested. During the long dinner he rose periodically to shout, "Everybody drink. Keep drinking."

Then began the tributes, handsomely suited to the master of the affectionate slam and the endearing defamation.

"You were a bum when you started," announced Baseball Commissioner Ford Frick. "You're a bum now. But you're a great bum and we like you."

"When Toots turned 50," recalled Red Smith of the *Herald Tribune*, "we all gathered here to weep great, big, slobbery tears for a fat, drunken saloonkeeper. We're doing the same tonight." Toots nodded approvingly.

Quentin Reynolds read a sentimental letter he had written for "Little Toots," the proprietor's 8-year-old son Rory, to open on his 21st birthday. . . . Reynolds got a standing ovation and Toots wept.

It was a remarkable document. Quent gave it his best reading:

Mr. Rory Shor
480 Park Avenue
New York, New York
Dear Rory:

When I have finished reading this short letter to your Father's friends, I am going to seal it. No one will see it until you open it on your 21st birthday, July 31, 1971. You're home in bed, kid, you're only 8½ years old and all of your Father's friends have gathered tonight to give him a party. But, let's not talk about that.

You're 21 today, Rory, and I guess no matter what you're doing, your pals ask you "Hey Rory, we've read a lot, and heard a lot about your old man. What's he really like?" That's a hard question to answer when you're 21, but maybe I can help you out.

Perhaps at school you studied the poetry and the books of Carl Sandburg. We think he's just about the best. Unfortunately, he's 84, and by the time you read this, he may be dead. Carl Sandburg writing about someone else, might well have been writing about your old man when he wrote:—

"Not often in the story of mankind does a man arrive on earth who is both steel and velvet, who is as hard as rock and soft as drifting fog."

Your Father is like that, Rory.

Seven hundred years ago, there lived a poet in Portugal named Poms Capdell. He wrote a thousand poems, but only two lines of his have survived. In the year 1245, he wrote:

"Oft have I heard and deemed the witness true
Whom man delights in, God delights in too."

He might have been writing about your Father too, Rory. In this room tonight, we have about three hundred of his friends, and another three hundred had to be turned away because we had no room.

In this room there are writers and boxers, actors and singers, businessmen and government officials. In this room there are saints and sinners, and they have all come to honor your Father. If the Almighty is looking down here tonight, He must feel delighted to see the warm affection that everyone in this room has for your old man. Yes, the old Portuguese poet might have been writing about him when he said "Whom man delights in, God delights in too."

I wonder if you've been to Ireland yet, Rory. If you go there, drop in to O'Malley's Bookstore in Dublin. It's just around the corner from the Shelbourne Hotel. I was there not long ago and I found an old book called merely *Irish Legends.* There's one short Irish legend I've never forgotten and I think it applies very well to your Father.

The Holiest man in Ireland was asked, "Who are the ones who are allowed into Heaven?" And he told them about three men who died the same day and found themselves outside the pearly gates. There were five angels sitting at a table, and their job was to investigate everyone who came before them. The first of the three newly arrived Irishmen said boldly, "I have spent a lifetime studying the Scriptures and have received many honors as the result of my learning. I certainly deserve to enter the pearly gates."

"Not so fast," the head angel said. "We have to investigate your motives."

The second man spoke up. "I spent most of my time on earth fasting, going to church, and mortifying the flesh."

"We will have to investigate your motives too," the head angel said. Then he turned to the third man and said, "Now what about you?"

The third man shrugged his shoulders and said, "I am no scholar and I never fasted, I missed church an awful lot of times and I don't know what this man means when he talks about mortifying the flesh. I'm just an innkeeper."

"How did you spend your time on earth?" the head angel asked curiously.

"Well," the man hesitated, "looking back, I didn't do much of anything. I lived a little, and I loved a little and I laughed a little. And . . . well, this is such a small thing it is hardly worth mentioning . . . but I always kept the door of my inn open and fed without charge every poor man who came by. I never turned away a man who was thirsty or hungry."

"That's enough," the head angel smiled. "No need to investigate you. Go right on in."

If the legend is true, Rory, and there's no reason to doubt it, they won't have to investigate your old man either. And that, Rory, is the kind of a guy he is.

Sincerely,
QUENTIN REYNOLDS

At last it was Toots's turn. He had rewritten the speech his literary friends had turned out for him. The final text, which he paraphrased and otherwise mutilated, probed unexplored recesses of the queen's English:

"There is nothing which is contrived by man as that which is produced at a good tavern or inn which is named a saloon and I know you fellows will agree with me.

"On Joe DiMaggio Day at Yankee Stadium, Joe said, 'I am lucky to be a Yankee.'

"When Leo Durocher quit the Polo Grounds, he said, 'I am lucky to be a Giant.'

"Sitting here looking at all you people, all I can say is, 'I am lucky to be a saloonkeeper.' I use and like the word saloon.

"All broadcasters always say, 'Stop at your favorite tavern.' I looked up the word tavern in the dictionary and the definition for a tavern is a gin mill with rooms upstairs. A saloon is more respectable.

"Since I opened this place in 1940, I feel not only my help are my friends but over a thousand regular customers—not only you fellows who live in New York but people from out of town who make this place their first stop. I feel I have over a thousand friends, and any man considers himself to have five or six friends but a saloonkeeper has the opportunity to meet a thousand and keep having them as friends.

"I would like to reminisce a little tonight. I don't feel like clowning or being funny. You have had plenty of laughs from the previous speakers. You fellows have made this night so important to me I want to be sentimental and tell you men that you are returning every favor I have ever done for anyone and, with plenty of interest! Most of us have had our ups and downs but I guess I have abused the privilege. It is no secret that I have been broke often but always some friend bailed me out. I went to banks and they laughed at me but my friends, never!! And there are men sitting in this room and elsewhere tonight who have said to me, 'What do you want,' and never said 'No.'

"How lucky for my family and me that my friends feel about me as I do about them.

"There is nothing I wouldn't do for a right guy and this wonderful night proves what you people would do for me.

"I will never forget the first night I opened this restaurant. I walked in flat broke without a penny. Jimmy Cannon walked over here with Baby and me and what a great nineteen years this has been!

"Even when things were at their roughest, every night was New Year's Eve around here. We were always drinking and being happy and the only sad occasions were when we lost one of our good pals. . . . God has been so good to me. . . . I have the most wonderful wife and children in the world. I have the greatest and most wonderful friends in the world. I love my job . . . running the most decent saloon I know.

"As I get older, I will tell my children stories about the very important men who lived in all walks of life and all the people who came into my store. . . . And their Pop was in such a good position to meet everybody. Through these doors have walked the greatest in sports, the greats of the industrial world, presidents, the high echelons of all religions, judges of all different courts and politicians. . . . And I have been fortunate because of your friendship and loyalty to this place to know them all intimately.

"This saloon isn't built of steel and bricks. . . . It is built of wonderful memories. This isn't a building being torn down, *it is me! When I sold this place, I only sold the steel and bricks because the memories were worth ten times of what I was paid for and nobody has enough money to buy the spirit of this place.* The companionship shows for itself here tonight.

"Some guys have money. I got you people and others for friends.

"I know that makes me the richest man in the world.

"All I can say forever to you fellows is . . . 'Thanks!'

"A lot of people think I am pretty smart or lucky getting a million and a half. It was nothing, anybody can do it. Just build a place in the middle of the block and wait for the right guy to come along.

"Funny, I never figured this place would have to be demolished. I thought on one of our good nights, the store would just collapse from an overload.

"Really, fellows, I feel terrible about pulling this saloon right out from under you, but I will be opening again one block to the north of Twenty-one and Rose's. At last, class will come to Fifty-second Street!

"Incidentally, while the joint is being built, I have a favor to ask all you dear, loyal, pals. Go to other places to drink. Never get in the habit of drinking at home, but, remember, where your real love is and always will be!

"You get a lot of advice when you are in a spot like me. People tell me to take it easy . . . to get a hobby. I tell them my hobby is drinking so I got to have a saloon therefore, everybody here knows I am going to work as hard as I possibly can to get this new place open as soon as possible."

Champlin's account in *Life* concluded: "Toots will open again one block north. But that will be months, maybe a year, from now. In the meantime, as one New York paper noted in alarm, thousands of bums will be homeless."

On the afternoon of the actual closing, a friend's column in the New York *Journal-American* pulled out all the stops:

Lower the Flag to half-mast and off with those hats, men. Keep those babbling children quiet, and arrest that fellow who's blowing his car horn. Instruct the towers at Idlewild and LaGuardia to reroute all air traffic to Philadelphia.

Somebody tell that black cat to stop purring. Push the button, Mayor, the one that turns all lights red and end the roaring traffic's boom. Plant a weeping willow in Times Square, and clap a derby on the trumpets in the 52nd Street gin-mills. Cut the cords on the ferry-boat whistles and muffle the massive oars of the *Queen Mary*.

Toots Shor's saloon closes tonight.

Fan the faint embers of memory and recall that every great town in every age had a saloon which served as a haven for those who sought companionship, comfort, or a quiet corner in which to lick a wound or douse a torch.

There are hieroglyphics in Cairo's Egyptian Museum that bespeak of Stone Age beer halls. In Pompeii, a marble slab that served as a wine bar bears the smooth concave marks dug through countless decades by the resting elbows of relaxing Romans. In the Piazza San Marco in Venice a saloon dating from the 1200's still thrives, as one does in Dante's town house in Rome, Hosteria Del Orso. In London's Fleet Street, pubs like Christopher Wren's Old Bell survive. The Cheshire Cheese hasn't changed much since Ben Jonson put down his pewter mug one clammy night, went up to his little frozen room, put a blanket around him, lighted his candle, and sticking a scrawny hand from under the blanket scratched a little rhyme which began, "Drink to me only with thine eyes/ and I will pledge with mine/

Leave but a kiss within the cup/ and I'll not ask for wine."

Toots Shor's saloon closes tonight.

Where will one now go to mourn a Ruth, a Corum, a Grantland Rice, a Hellinger, a Robert Sherwood? It was usually a nonstop flight from the funeral of a pal to this place of which I sing. The proprietor considered drink a part of the liturgy of a requiem, a kind of incense whose fragrance was calculated to speed the departed spirit to his reward.

And he was his own best mourner. He suffered what his competitors felt was a stroke of madness the night Roosevelt died. He shut the joint, though he needed the money. His place was an oddly fitting frame for immense sorrow in the wake of a wake, and nobody was more affected than he. Bugs Baer undertook the unnerving job of getting him to Campbell's to see the mortal remains of his friend Jimmy Walker and later said of the ordeal, "Getting Toots to the funeral parlor was like towing a sick whale with no hope of ambergris."

Toots Shor's saloon closes tonight.

It was a stage for burlesque, too, one that echoed the bellows of a Gleason and the razory observations of a Fred Allen. Oddly, there weren't many fights, for a predominantly male saloon. Tom O'Reilly, a gentle sportswriter, pushed Bobo Newsom, a large baseball pitcher, over a table one night. But it was largely a case of mistaken identity. O'Reilly thought he (O'Reilly) was somebody else.

Toots Shor's saloon closes tonight.

If there is to be a tablet to mark where it stood, or a time capsule, let it recall that on this spot men with no money in their pockets spent pity on a millionaire, comforted him as the bulldozer clanked toward a door which had known the scratchings of wolves. They wept with him over the cruel turn of events that had brought him riches but no immediate base of operations. They shared his sorrow as he was crowned with the ultimate tragedy of success, but without a stage on which to take a bow.

Toots Shor's saloon closes tonight.

Jiminy crickets . . .

Toots paid off $300,000 he still owed on 51 West 51, and a quarter of a million to his Jersey partners and the estate of Leo Justin. Clearly, what he must now do was to find a new location and build as quickly as possible. Could he swing 33 West 52d, where he had bounced for Leon and Eddie? Where would he raise the dough?

So he reacted strongly to the crisis and challenge, somewhat typically: "Pack up, Husky," he said. "We're going to Europe."

ABOVE LEFT: Toots, Bugs Baer, Robert L. Ripley and George Rector attack an outsized salami. ABOVE RIGHT: With Marilyn Monroe and her husband Joe. BELOW: Toots with President Truman and Richard E. Berlin, chairman of the Hearst Corporation

Beauties and the Beast: Toots with Paulette Goddard and Loretta Young

ABOVE: With two of his all-time giants: Mrs. John J. McGraw and
Mel Ott. BELOW: Toots had some Texas friends, too: Gov. Allan
Shivers, far left, and an up-and-coming congressman named Lyndon
B. Johnson.

ABOVE LEFT: Toots offends Chef Aime De Plante by passing judgment on the soup. ABOVE RIGHT: Nobody could guess who Toots was trying to imitate this night in his joint—not even his good friend David Shelley, who was imitating a waiter. BELOW: At Madison Square Garden—Toots is the one on top.

ABOVE LEFT: The Shors with their late great admirer, Edward R. Murrow. ABOVE RIGHT: The long and short of it: Toots with Eddie Arcaro, who would give him two shots a hole. BELOW LEFT: Toots and the Duke of Windsor, the Duchess and their friend, financier Charles Cushing, with Baby on the far right—apparently all feeling a bit upset over Toots's hoist of the former Defender of the Faith. BELOW RIGHT: Toots will back any proposition that says Rocky Graziano and Tony Zale were two of the greatest fighters who ever did battle.

"Me and Joe"

BELOW LEFT: His Honor Robert Wagner runs into Toots, or vice versa. BELOW RIGHT: Last photo taken of Toots with his old teeth

Toots and some baseball immortals at Shor's: (left to right, back) Jimmy Foxx, Mel Ott, Mickey Cochrane, Ed Walsh, Toots, Rogers Hornsby, Pie Traynor, Tris Speaker; (front) Fred Clarke, Arlie

Latham, Cy Young, George Sisler, Charley Nichols, Ty Cobb, and Charley Gehringer

ABOVE: Hitherto unpublished photo of Toots Shor warming up for his trip to Europe, after selling his joint for $1,500,000. BELOW: Living it up—at Maxim's in Paris: Virginia Warren Daly, Toots, Baby, Art Buchwald and owner Louis Vaudable

Toots the Family Man, circa 1957, with Tracey on his lap and, to his left, Rory, Mrs. Shor and Kerry. Bari Ellen is in gingham.

ABOVE: Four regulars on the Toots Shor A.C. ball club—Leo Durocher, Frank Sinatra, Toots (manager) and Joe DiMaggio. BELOW: Toots gives Averell Harriman some much-needed advice—on a horse. Harriman appears to be skeptical.

BILL MARK

Above: Toots in the locker room at Baltusrol, New Jersey, with the pro he feels was the toughest of them all—Ben Hogan. Below: Toots at the ground breaking of his restaurant at 33 W. 52, with two rock crushers, Jackie Gleason and Jack Dempsey

JACK SHARIN

CHAPTER 5

"All I've done is exchange saloons. . . ."

JOHN DALY was named by concerned mutual friends to brief Toots on how to conduct himself on his first European trip. Toots must be above all discreet, John told him with a straight face. He must remain sober even in the face of vicissitude. He must not disparagingly compare what he experienced or ate or drank overseas with what he was accustomed to at home. He must be restrained in his language. He must not call anybody in the old country a creepy bum. He should at least attempt to spend a few minutes examining the available cultural wonders. "You must remember that you're a kind of ambassador from the United States, you slob," Toots's chief of protocol crisply ordered. "A certain number of people will recognize your name and observe your deportment. Don't give the United States a bad name."

Others interested in the welfare of the United States also spoke to Toots before he took off on Pan Am with Baby and Baby's traveling companion, Chief Justice Warren's daughter Virginia. Among the concerned were Earl Wilson, a seasoned traveler, and several unseasoned ones: Yogi Berra, Whitey Ford, and Mickey Mantle. Speaking to Art Buchwald in Paris about this ordeal, Toots said:

"I'm a bum who likes booze, and those crums thought I'd get drunk and raise hell over here and make a scene. Somebody told me they even got hold of J. Edgar Hoover and asked him if he could keep me from coming over here but Hoover said, 'Let the crum go.'

"So for two weeks before I'm ready to go everyone is calling me up and saying, Toots, be a good American, don't cause no trouble, you're wearing the American flag on your

g List for Order #058-5040865-7569133

to

. De Fiore
ımond Circle
ey, PA 18034

rmation

e: 07/23/2006
Anthony E. De Fiore c/o Mary Ann Orgler
ed: Standard

ısidine, Bob
i96839210

3F308020
35902330649003

tion

book2
.book@gte.net

ng on Amazon Marketplace. Please be sure to rate your experience with this seller by visiting
ı/feedback. View more information about this seller at www.amazon.com/seller/jerobook2.

chest, and stuff like that. Everyone says no matter what happens I shouldn't get in a beef with anyone and I should say yes to everything. Well, I figure these guys are really concerned about me leaving the country, so I'll take their advice. After all, as long as I can get good booze I'm not going to cause anybody any trouble.

"The plane was supposed to go to Rome but instead we got stuck in Shannon. Baby starts buying out the entire 1959 Irish linen production. I tell her that we're going to have a tough time carrying all that stuff around Europe, and it's going to cost us five hundred dollars overweight. She's of Irish descent, so she says, 'I've got to help my people.' Well, I start to yell in the airport store when she says to me, 'You're behaving like an ugly American.' Immediately, I shut up. After all, I promised all those bums in New York.

"Now I'm in Rome and everybody's treating me real good and laying on the wine because they think that since I'm a big American restaurateur I'm an expert. What they don't know is for the whole time I was operating my joint I've got, say, three bottles of wine in the cellar and I couldn't even sell them. The bums that came to my place drank booze and beer. But every time somebody drags out the *vino* in Rome I say yes, but I'm getting sick to my stomach because I don't dig the grapes.

"We go to Florence and I'm saying yes to my wife all the time in public. This costs me like fifteen hundred dollars. But I know the guys back home are going to be proud of me because I'm not making a scene.

"We move on to Venice. It's raining the whole time, but I'm not complaining. The Italians got a right to rain like anybody else and as a good American all I can do is wish them luck. From Venice we're supposed to drive to Milan to catch a plane for Paris. The chauffeur asks if we want to stop in Padua for lunch as we have plenty of time. I say yes. He asks if he can visit his relatives in Padua for lunch. I say yes. Then he wants to drive by his old school and see how it looks. I say yes. So we blow the plane in Milan by fifteen minutes.

"I'm ready to let this bum have it when a vision of Bernard Baruch comes before my eyes, saying 'Remember, Toots, you are a goodwill ambassador.' So I thank this bum for the wonderful drive and we take a plane out for Zurich which is supposed to connect with a plane to Paris. But when we get to Zurich there's no room on the plane to Paris. The man there says it was all a mistake and he knows I'll understand. I say yes.

"The next day we make it to Paris. There are no taxis at the airport except the one I'm heading for with the girls. But this Frenchman pushes me aside and gets in with his wife. I bring back my fist, but Baby starts whistling 'The Star-Spangled Banner,' and I let the French bum get away.

"So I finally get to the hotel and that night I go out to hear the gypsy violinists in Montmartre. They start opening bottles of champagne like there was no tomorrow, and what makes it worse is they're piling up the empties from the other tables under mine. The violinists are all drinking my champagne and before I leave I get a tab for two hundred dollars.

"I'm now ready to wreck the joint when suddenly I hear John Daly's voice, like it's coming over a loudspeaker: 'Whatever you do, Toots, remember it's their country and they have their customs. They may seem strange to us but our customs are strange to them also.' So I pay the bill and even after I give a tip, they're throwing the empties at me as I leave the joint.

"As I'm getting into a cab—I notice the meter's been running for three days, maybe—I can't take it any more. As the cab is pulling away from the curb I yell at the headwaiters, 'You creepy bums!'

"Baby pulls me back in the cab and says, 'As your wife I can understand you acting so rudely, but as an American citizen I'm truly shocked.' "

In Rome, Toots's prime chronicler was Jack Casserly, then chief of the Hearst Headline Service bureau there. Casserly wrote:

"Toots Shor is the only tourist who ever came to Rome with an English dictionary. When he took his first look at Rome his immediate reaction was 'That Caesar was a great bum.' But he soon became footsore: 'They ought to rename this town Stepsville,' he said. 'We've never climbed more steps in our lives. I've personally climbed more steps than Casey Stengel did last season, taking out his pitchers.' "

Toots joined a few before him, excepting Martin Luther, who had flipped over St. Peter's.

"Talk about history, beauty, and feeling," he said to Casserly. "At St. Peter's you just stand there without a word. You look. There's nothing you can say. Nobody can write a vocabulary for it."

Jack asked him if anything else had deeply moved him in Rome.

"Yeah," Toots said. "I saw a church with two statues out in front. On one side is the statue of St. Patrick. On the other side there's a statue, so help me, to a saint named Isadore. How about that? All Broadway ought to see it."

Toots had a special audience with Pope John XXIII but found he had only one thing in common with the Pontiff: their dimensions. He kept a stream of postcards, cables, and phone calls squirting back at his chums in New York and Hollywood. He was homesick. Thus Leonard Lyons was able to report: "In Paris, Toots listened to friends advise him about Maxim's. Yes, he'll go there. Tour d'Argent? No. 'I can't pronounce that,' said Toots. 'Why should I go to places if I can't tell people where I been?' " Earl Wilson caught up with a postcard Toots sent to Jackie Gleason. It was a picture of the ruins of the Colosseum. "I'll work on the rest of it tomorrow," Toots had written. Wilson also reported that Toots must have had a gay time on the Pan Am plane going over. The wire he sent to Wilson, announcing his arrival, bore a notation by the telegrapher: "Signature indistinctly written."

Toots had saved London for the last, but his stay there had overtones of the frustration Babe Ruth had suffered some years before in Paris. Babe somehow expected to have every French girl from sixteen to sixty throw herself at him. He had seen enough movies about them to expect that. On his first day there he climbed into his familiar camel's hair coat and cap, made up some improbable excuse to his wife Clair to the effect that he had business to attend to, and set off jauntily for the Champs Élysées. He returned hours later and sat down, exhausted, on the side of his bed.

"What's the matter, honey?" his wife asked him.

Babe shook his head.

"Nobody gave a damn," Babe said.

Toots' chief frustration in London was the language barrier.

"The British people talk like a guy in a chimney," he later complained to Murray Robinson of the *Journal-American*. "London was the only place I had any trouble understanding. They couldn't understand me neither. And how about the way they drink? They close the bars from three to six P.M.! Now that hurts a habit like mine. It knocks a big hole in a man's drinking day."

The most searching attention Fleet Street paid to Toots was by Patricia Lewis of the *Daily Express*. She frightened Toots a bit by inviting him to her apartment, for the beginning of the interview, and offering him a martini.

"Imagine drinking a bomb with a strange broad at ten o'clock in the morning!" he was to say later in his best shocked manner. They chastely moved on to Simpson's, the Strand's most venerated roast beef place, where Toots immediately felt more at home. A scanning of Miss Lewis' subsequent interview, as printed in Lord Beaverbrook's paper, indicated that Toots must have still been shaken by the near miss of the martini—a drink he considers lethal. He resorted to two of his chief security blankets: whiskey and prominent friends. Toots is not a man to drop a drink, but the names of friends drop easily from his lips when he needs the solace of their sounds.

He spoke of drinking at Siegi's, London's popular sports-minded bar.

"All I've done is exchange saloons, but it feels good," he said. "The booze is the same. I guess I'm happy anywhere, s'long as there's a good bar," Miss Lewis quoted him, perhaps detecting a slight slur—rare in Toots's speech at that time of day.

" 'Through the years I made a lotta friends,' the *Daily Express* story continued. 'That's the secret of life, friends. One was a guy called Mark Hellinger, a writer. He intro-

duced me to Billy LaHiff, who ran Damon Runyon's hang-
out, the Tavern. I took over and ran the place till in 1936
I bought it . . . with the same guys in there all the time.'

"But if you live like Toots Shor," Miss Lewis wrote, "you
find that as you come up so you go down. In 1939 he lost
the Tavern in a gambling debt." Showing little mercy, she
continued:

" 'I was broke again, but somehow with the help of friends
I recovered and a year later I opened Toots Shor's. You see
what I mean about friends? A cop can stop me for speedin'.
We have a word . . . and that's that. Friends, y'see? And
the people who made my place, the sportswriters, the columnists, the guys like DiMaggio and Joe Louis and Sinatra,
they came there because it was a place they'd know their
friends would be.

" 'So many people don't do anything about friends until
a guy dies and then they go to the wake. Why not have
a drink with 'em while they're livin'? Me? I'm strictly a
booze man.' "

Toots was somewhat indignant about the interview after
his return to New York.

"In her story the broad says 'he maneuvered his seventeen
stone into London,' he told Murray Robinson. "What kind
of crack is that? It sounds like they keep track of how many
times I got loaded. Well, I got stoned a lot more times than
seventeen before I got to London."

He had assured Miss Lewis that martinis were a potion
of the Devil's making and that he, Toots, not Lucifer, was
totally uninterested in food. She nailed him pretty good on
both counts.

"For a noneating man, Mr. Shor seemed strangely at
home with smoked trout, oysters, beef, two cheeses, a large
dry martini, and two carafes of wine," she recorded to her
millions of readers throughout the empire.

"That was smoked salmon, not trout," Toots complained
to Robinson. 'I know lox when I eat it. But their oysters
are very good, I must say. They eat them plain. When I
open my joint on Fifty-second Street in about seven months,
I'm gonna introduce plain oysters."

Toots, who had booked a bet or two in his past, marveled
at the casual manner in which the British called their book-
makers while lunching and bet on a horse.

"It'd be Katy-bar-the-door, if anything like that happened
in New York," he assured his British friend, Gus Newman
and his American wife, the former Frances Moody of Gal-
veston, at the Savoy Grill one day over a small hatchery
of plovers' eggs and room-temperature lager. He had to be
thinking of the Tavern.

Toots retains mixed feelings about his discovery of Europe.

"Maybe I didn't help international relations, but I didn't
hurt them either," he says with becoming modesty. "I got
taken here and there. For example, I blew my beret. I did
my part in keeping our friendship with those foreigners,
but I still got a beef when some crum over there didn't
do his. Like the bum who stole my beret. I got it from a
guy just before I left for there. He said, 'Here, we want
you to look like the dashing *boulevardier* in Paris, don't
we? So put on this dicer and practice good before you get
over there.' Then one day over there it's gone. I must've
been sober at the time because it's a well-known fact that
you can't roll a drunk."

(Toots ignored a friend's comment that, in a beret, he
looked like a diseased mushroom.)

He found the British the most honest of all the curious
foreigners he met, but feels that at least one representative
of that curious species took him for a sucker.

"Cabdriver," Toots explained. "The guy says to me, 'If
you're a visitor you must be sure to see the Old Lady of
Threadneedle Street in the City.' I said okay. But it turned
out to be nothing. Just a bunch of banks."

La Lewis discovered enough of Toots to make a two-part
series titled "Things My Mother Never Taught Me." The
subtitle for the second article was "How to Handle the Hard-
Drinking Kind of Man." She had a previous brush with
Toots, she revealed:

"I tasted autumn in New York for the first time a year ago.
It was wild! It was wonderful! And I came to frequent a

certain pub on 51st street that seemed the favourite place to meet the more amusing people in town."

That would have been Toots's.

Other gems from her de Toqueville scrutiny of Toots:

"Because he is a man who knows more about life as it is lived and the people who make it rich than most others, I sought him out. I found the rumbustious Mr. Shor, not unnaturally, in a bar.

" 'Hell,' he roared, 'This is my first time in Europe, but it feels good—the booze is the same. Y'know the only thing I don't like over here are these saloon-keepers who put on a black tie and call themselves rest-aur-a-teurs.' Mr. Shor minced a few steps to punctuate the word. 'Jeez! I've had four Presidents in my saloon and I don't call myself no rest-aur-a-teur.'

". . . Arriving at Simpsons in the Strand—where the bar is regular and the beef is rare—Mr. Shor gazed at the huge roasts wheeled in on silver trolleys.

" 'Ay say,' he quipped to the head waiter. 'Jolly good fun, what d'you say? Bung ho and all that jazz!'

"For a moment it was touch and go whether we'd be thrown out, but my friend relieved the situation by distributing currency with Texan largesse around the room.

" 'This is a masculine-type place,' he observed. 'You know dolls like to go to a man's place but guys don't like to go to a dolls' place.'

"I conceded Mr. Shor an excellent point and asked him to expand.

" 'Well, the main thing for a person is never to forget where they came from,' rumbled Toots. 'I left Philly (Philadelphia) in 1929 and I left broke and in disgust. So I went to New York and got me a job in a speakeasy. I was a tough kid and they used me as a bouncer. Then I was at the Cotton Club up in Harlem one night—I recall that Lena Horne was in the chorus—Boy! What a line up!'

"I dragged Toots back to the subject.

" 'Through the years I made a lotta friends—and that's the secret of life, friends.'

Looking back on the trip as a whole, Toots is philosophical.

He would like to have seen his friends Lucky Luciano and
Joe Adonis while in Naples, but the exiled hoods told him
by phone that it wouldn't look very nice if they were seen
in the company of a visiting group that included the daughter of Chief Justice Warren. He did see Orson Welles in
Paris, an expatriate he had hardly seen since the days of the
Tavern and the Mercury Players. They fell upon each other
like affectionate hippos. Finally, to Toots's relief, he was
given what he felt was the right to hit a foreigner. That
happy moment came in Harry's Bar, in Venice.

"Some greasy bum we didn't know reached over the table
and started to light Ginny's cigarette," he related on coming home. "I gave him a chop on his arm. I growled at him.
I said, 'Get out! Where we come from, ladies light their
own cigarettes!' He ran."

Sometimes, in retrospect, Toots sums up the grand tour
in a single sentence: "I'm probably the only bum who went
to Europe and came back as ignorant as when he left."

CHAPTER 6

"I never once saw Spelly at the bar."

THE laughter died down a month after Toots's return. Arnold Grant called him and said, "You might as well know. Zeckendorf is broke. Forget that place he was going to help you with on Fifty-second Street and start looking around for a new spot."

Zeckendorf had already built a million-dollar hole for the foundation of his multi-multimillion-dollar forty-eight storied hotel and had plans and high hopes for a seven-storied garage on 52d Street. The building was also to house the new Toots Shor's. A tunnel running under 52d Street would connect hotel, garage, and Toots's.

Toots's dreams went glimmering and, with them temporarily his best chance of striking oil—inexhaustible oil—again. He bears no malice because he shares so many of Zeckendorf's colorful traits.

"I feel sorry for Bill," says the man Bill feels sorry for. "He's a great crapshooter. Jiminy crickets, the dough he's gone through! But he's never let it get him down. He keeps swinging. You see him riding around town in a big car with a chauffeur, and even a big dog." Toots has only a small dog.

Toots took Grant's advice and started looking around.

"Grant went to Japan on a vacation right after he gave me the bad news," Toots says, "so I looked around on my own. Maybe that's my trouble. I should have had somebody with me like Leo Justin. If Leo had lived, I never would have had any money troubles."

It turned out to be a long look. For those who trudged along with him, a good portion of the search seemed to be done in 21, the Colony, Moore's, Gallagher's, Lawton Carver's, Rose's, the Waldorf's Bull and Bear, Nicky Blair's Blair House, and other well-known real-estate agencies.

With the notable exceptions of 21, the Stork Club, Pavillon and, say, the Racquet Club, almost every bar and restaurant in New York would have liked to have had Toots's services during what eventually became a more than two-year interregnum. He was offered hosting positions at a dozen well-known places. The Taft Hotel tried to lure him with a promise that it would redecorate its grill room to make it a replica of Toots's now-razed place on 51st Street. Toots would have nothing of that.

Toots kept looking, sometimes actually at building sites. After Grant returned, Grant looked too. There was not a very good rapport between them; either that or they were using different maps. They invited a reporter to have a drink with them one day at the Drake Hotel on Park Avenue, after which they would show him the site for the new Toots Shor's. After the drink, the three walked out of the Drake. "It's this way," Toots and Grant said simultaneously.

Grant walked east. Toots walked west. The reporter just stood there, looking more puzzled than ever. Grant had decided on a place on Park Avenue in the Fifties; Toots had honed in on a building just west of the Drake, toward Madison.

The confusion of that period sometimes spread to the places Toots frequented during the booze-and-food breaks in his search for the ultimate roost. It was not easy for Toots to become a docile customer after so many years of being the unquestioned and infallible boss. He ordered a good customer to leave Blair's one night or be thrown out. He kept forgetting he wasn't in charge. At Duke Zeibert's place in Washington a Florida sportsman named Bill McDonald joined the table where Toots was having a happy time with sportswriters Shirley Povich, Bob Addie, Moe Siegel, Bert Hawkins, and several others. The wealthy man had come to town to buy Harry Wismer's 25 percent share of the Washington Redskins. He lumbered into a chair at

Toots's invitation ("I thought it would be a good chance for him to meet the Washington sportswriters").

Both Toots and McDonald had just come to Zeibert's separately from a Democratic party fund-raising affair at the Mayflower. Toots had turned down an invitation from the Kennedy brothers, Jack and Bobby, to stay for dinner. Now he was glad he had. McDonald told two stories that would have curled a mule skinner's beard. Toots was morally outraged, which he enjoys.

"Don't use words like that," Toots said to him quietly. "There are ladies sitting here with us."

The man, now mercifully gone to his reward, said he didn't mind talking any way he derned pleased in front of no sportswriter or no sportswriter's wife or daughter because all sportswriters were crooked anyway. "On the take," is the way he put it. That went particularly, he added, for Bill Corum.

There was a shocked pause at the table, broken finally by Toots.

"Step outside," Toots said, standing up.

The guy wouldn't go. It might have been Toots's finest hour, but he was deprived of it. He searched for something equally devastating.

"You piece of raisin cake, you're barred from my joint," Toots said, distilling instant and terrible anathema.

"You don't have one," the guy said, which should have left Toots for dead, but didn't.

"If I ever get one, you're barred!" Toots roared. Those present considered it the finest hypothetical topper of the season.

(When George Preston Marshall, principal owner of the Redskins heard about the incident, he would not let the $350,000 worth of stock * go to the man Toots had barred. He deflected it, instead, to Jack Kent Cooke. "I don't want to be a partner with anybody who knocks Bill Corum," he said. He and Corum had been friends for years, both being swingers. Corum wrote many columns about Marshall and his dazzling flamboyance, including one that began "George

---

* It is now valued at $3 million.

Preston Marshall slipped unobtrusively into town today leading a 100-piece brass band.")

Toots's favorite restaurant during his long layoff was 21.
He enjoyed three things about it: (1) the food, (2) making
the Kriendlers and the Bernses nervous, and (3) denouncing
the stiff prices. He continued to live by his creed that there
is no such thing as overtipping, but he was incensed one
day to learn that 21 was charging him $1.25 for bread and
butter he never ordered. That had been a custom of the
house for many years. Toots objected on the ground that
where he was concerned this was a violation of professional
ethics. He never has gotten over it.

"When I was out of action they treated me like a customer, not like a friend," he sometimes says, with massive
self-pity.

From the start of his wanderings, Toots sensed that eventually he would wind up on the site of Leon and Eddie's. It
was a case of water and whiskey finding its natural level.
The prodigal's return was inevitable but the path was thorny.
There had been a period during which Toots believed in his
optimistic way that Zeckendorf would more or less present
the property to him on a platinum platter. Now the hard-
pressed land gambler said he would be happy to sell it
for only $1.75-million, Toots being a good friend. Toots
scraped up what was left of his $1.5-million, borrowed the
difference, and took control. But much more was needed
if the dream of a big garage with restaurant enclosed was
to come true. Prudential offered to lend him $2.7-million.
Toots, who didn't have $270 in walking-around money, shook
his head. It wasn't enough.

It was about this time that his friend Harold Gibbons
of St. Louis suggested that Toots take his case to the Teamsters' Union Pension Fund. Gibbons was and is a top-echelon
man in the Teamsters. He is a tall, good-looking, distinguished gentleman who looks about as much like an associate of Jimmy Hoffa as does Clark Clifford. A date was
arranged and Toots went to Washington to face the all-

powerful bantam boss of the biggest (1,666,000 members) labor union in history.

"Hello, Toots," Hoffa said as Gibbons led him in.

"Hi'ya, Jimmy," Toots said, shaking hands. They had never seen each other. But it was "Jimmy" and "Toots" from the start. It stayed that way after Hoffa went to prison. Jail doesn't represent a stigma to Toots as long as he's convinced that his friend got a bum rap. At St. Patrick's Cathedral for the funeral of Bradley Kelly, long-time King Features Syndicate executive, Toots was recognized and greeted by a total stranger. Toots sighed happily and whispered, "You know something? I'm known best at sports events, saloons, churches, synagogues, and jails. I know so many people in them."

Hoffa made up his mind swiftly after sizing up the towering petitioner from New York. He told the Pension Fund board that Toots looked trustworthy and the Fund was lucky to be able to invest in him. The vote was, of course, unanimous.

One of Toots's first acts of celebration was to put in a call to a reporter friend who was in Honolulu at the time.

"I got the money, I got the money!" he shouted over the five thousand miles. "I got the money from the Teamsters."

The friend said, "Oh."

"What's wrong with that?" Toots demanded.

"It's okay, I guess," the friend said, after a bit. "At least you won't have to worry about a name for the joint. You can call it Toots Shor's Hoffabrau."

"Very funny, you creepy big-nosed bum," he said. "All the fund does is okay me and I get the dough from Chase Manhattan."

"And you get Hoffa standing at the bar every day," the friend said over the long wire.

"He don't drink," Toots said.

"All right, suppose he just stands there having a Coke?"

There was a slab of silence from the East Coast of the United States.

"I'm still not worried," Toots finally said. "The New York

archdiocese had a mortgage for a time on my other joint, but I never once saw Spelly at the bar."

The ground breaking was the biggest opening New York had had since *South Pacific*. It had a more distinguished cast than Mary Martin and Ezio Pinza. It had the Chief Justice of the United States Supreme Court, Mickey Mantle, Jackie Gleason, Whitey Ford, Ed Sullivan, Phil Harris, Phil Silvers, Billy Conn, Kyle Rote, Jack Dempsey, Yogi Berra, Jim Farley, former mayor of New York Bill O'Dwyer, Baseball Commissioner Ford Frick, Bobby Feller, George Jessel, Attorney General Louis Lefkowitz, a brazen Dixieland band, a groaning buffet table, and a Gold Rush bar, all housed under a circus sideshow tent, appropriately enough.

Little Rory Shor, shyly proud in his construction worker's hard hat, scooped the first shovelful. His father beamed.

"All these crum bums will one day be your customers," Toots said of the Chief Justice and the others who had assembled.

Gleason, watching the boy dig, vociferously observed, "It took them six months to scrape the grease out of Toots's old kitchen." As the big earth mover took over and clawed half a ton of dirt from the site, Jackie explained, "Toots's kid lost his ball." Commenting on the weather—it was a chilly October 7, 1960—Gleason said, "Toots finally got his air-conditioning working." Or did Jessel say that? Or Lee Meyers? Or Peter Donald? Or John Daly?

The alignment of 21, Toots's, and Rose's gave Gleason an idea.

"It's a great arrangement," he told Toots. "We'll first go to Twenty-one and meet some nice people. Then get drunk in your place. And then eat in Rose's." Jessel said he had checked with the Kriendlers to see if they were miffed at Toots for locating next door to 21. "They're not sore at all, Toots, they're grateful," George reported. "They said, 'Good. It'll be a place for our chauffeurs to eat.'" During the party one of the guests had a parking ticket slapped on his windshield.

He asked Chief Justice Warren to fix it. "You're a judge, aren't you?"

It was that sort of happy day.

But a long and often dreary year was to pass before Toots's new place opened. It took some doing. It took also somewhere between $5-million and $6-million of the Teamsters' money. Opening day was delayed, among other reasons, by a twelve-week strike—by the teamsters. Toots was justifiably proud of his place and of the famed architect Charlie Luckman, who had duplicated the mellow brick and wood paneling mood of the old place so successfully that eventually the resident storytellers often couldn't remember whether Gleason passed out at 51 West 51 or 33 West 52.

There were a number of previews of the new place, including a Yankee free load for baseball writers and officials for the showing of the Lew Fonseca's official films of the 1961 World Series between the Yankees and the Cincinnati Reds. Much was written about the occasion, but Bill Slocum of the New York *Mirror,* who was given a private preview of the joint, gave his readers an in-depth report:

> Shor turns his waiters and himself loose on a helpless public come Wednesday, but in the meantime he is rehearsing all concerned with his new bistro.
>
> I heard his brave words of self-sacrifice to his embattled waiters by the sheerest of accident. In fact, I eavesdropped shamelessly. I was being taken on an inspection tour when we entered one of the great halls below decks. Here these waiters, a captive audience if ever I saw one, were listening to the rolling Oxonian accents of T. Bernard.
>
> Perhaps 10 were familiar faces left over from the old joint. The remaining 40 were strangers and they listened to T. Bernard as if they had never heard anything like this before. As indeed, they hadn't.
>
> The Winston Churchill of the saloons said to his waiters, "You will be privileged to serve some of the great men of our times, fellows who can hit .300 in the majors, great football players, main event prize fighters. Important people."

I noticed a delicate shudder of distaste sweep several of the old timers among the waiters. Shor looks on athletes as demi-gods, to be served and adored. His veteran waiters look on athletes as lousy tippers to be avoided, shunned, ignored.

"As for the other customers," Sir Toots went on, "don't take no lip from any of them. Just because some crum bum owns a big advertising agency or wrote a best seller don't mean he has any right to interfere with service for, let's say, Whitey Ford, if he's here. Keep them square crums in their place and if any of them beefs let me know. I'll throw him out personally."

Later Toots received me graciously in his office for tea. He spoke of his theories in running an international example of haute cuisine.

"I don't permit no garlic in nothing," he said. "I further don't permit no dishes on the menu I can't pronounce. That cuts down on the choices available, but I got a new French chef. I don't know how good he can cook yet, but he translates into small American words real good."

He showed me a closed circuit TV screen. "I can sit up here in my office and watch everything down there," he proclaimed. "I don't have to mingle with the customers. That's got to be great for business."

He speaks much truth.

The new place will be opened to athletes and squares come Wednesday at fourish. Milord plans no party. Just a simple mass opening for the peasantry in the true baronial tradition.

Oddly, at that very moment there will be a party next door in "21." That's where Shor has spent a large part of the two years he was without his own saloon. A spokesman at "21" said, "We are celebrating the fact that Mr. Shor now has a place of his own to run. The party will give us an opportunity to explain to our newer employees that Mr. Shor does not own "21" no matter what impressions they and he have had for the last two years.

"We wish Mr. Shor only the best. In fact, we do hope he will be very, very busy."

Jimmy Cannon of the *Journal American* escorted Baby to opening night, December 27, 1961. It was a date he had made with her the night the old joint closed, two and a half years before. He had been present at her unheralded arrival at the opening of the first place. Jimmy wrote:

"This time Baby wore a mink coat. We arrived in a chauffeur-driven limousine with their four children. No one was on the sidewalk 20 years ago. But now the photographers took Baby's picture.

" 'Just a minute,' she said. She fished in her purse and carefully counted out 40 cents. Then she threw it into the street. The coins rolled in the slush and were pursued by kids who forgot their autograph books.

" 'For luck,' she said."

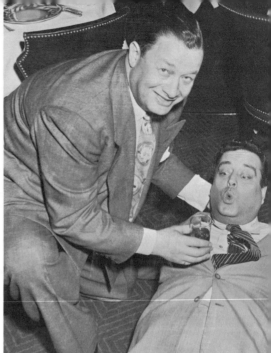

ABOVE LEFT: Chief Justice Earl Warren was the first head of the Supreme Court ever to help launch the ground breaking of a saloon. He was happy to be aboard. He and Toots have been friends for years. ABOVE RIGHT: Toots administering artificial respiration to Jackie Gleason. BELOW LEFT: Toots makes it back to 33 W. 52 after breaking his leg in Washington. BELOW RIGHT: Rory Shor, demonstrating his legitimacy

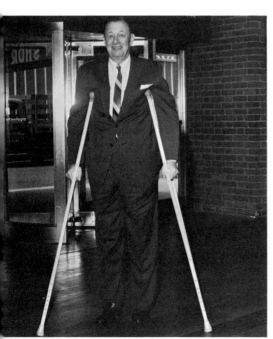

ABOVE: Ugly scene near men's room. BELOW: Seymour Weiss, Jimmy Durante, Walter Winchell, Joe E. Lewis and Toots

OPPOSITE PAGE: Toots always thought he was a pretty big guy until he met Wilt Chamberlain. ABOVE LEFT: Francis, Cardinal Spellman and friend, taken at Shor's when the Cardinal attended a luncheon given by Mickey Mantle. ABOVE RIGHT: Ecumenism in action: Toots and Monsignor William J. McCormack, whose father once offered to give $1,000,000 to charity if Toots gave up drinking. BELOW: Toots and Baby with Mr. and Mrs. Ken Venturi, who appeared on Ed Sullivan's TV show after Ken won the National Open.

BILL MARK   MAX PETER HAAS

ABOVE LEFT: General Motors Vice-President Anthony De Lorenzo and Toots with their friend Terence, Cardinal Cooke. ABOVE RIGHT: Old pals—Ethel Merman and Toots. BELOW LEFT: The chief reason for the laughter here is that neither Shor nor Considine can drop a one-foot putt under pressure. BELOW RIGHT: Toots plays chauffeur for the newlyweds, Debbie Considine and Lt. Karl Hoyo, at the Deal Golf and Country Club, Deal, New Jersey.

ABOVE: Toots went to the White House to see his friend, center, give the office of Undersecretary of Labor to James J. Reynolds, younger brother to Quent. BELOW: Lee Iacocca, founding father of Ford's Mustang, and South Africa's Gary Player, waiting with Toots to go to the head table at William Denis Fugazy's annual All American Collegiate Golf Champions Dinner

Toots flattens Jack Dempsey and strangles Gene Tunney at a sports banquet. For an encore, he falls on Lowell Thomas.

ABOVE: Toots with Mrs. Bing Crosby and a former drinking companion, Mr. Crosby. BELOW: He never had a prouder night than this one, with two of the all-time greats of baseball, his friends Mickey Mantle and Willie Mays.

ABOVE, CLOCKWISE: Toots discussing his diet with movie mogul Joe Levine and comedian Marty Allen. That's Gleason, peek-a-booing. Toots and Audrey Meadows Six, the former Mrs. Ralph Kramden. The proprietor wound up one happy night with Bob Hope, William Denis Fugazy and Vic Damone. BELOW: The Great Gleason has some crushing comment to make about Shor, which William Randolph Hearst, Jr., considers most amusing.

ABOVE LEFT: Joey Adams, Earl Wilson, a somewhat truculent-looking proprietor, and a docile Manassa Mauler, Jack Dempsey, meet at a March of Dimes Dinner honoring Harry Hershfield. ABOVE RIGHT: Toots advising attorney Eugene Foley, one of Vice President Hubert Humphrey's 1968 campaign managers, on just how to defeat Richard Nixon

BELOW LEFT: Toots and John Wayne—hatching a new plot against their common foe: Geronimo. BELOW CENTER: Beautiful Julie Wilson brushes off Toots. BELOW RIGHT: Toots and Willie Shoemaker—a study in physiological contrasts

BILL MARK   BILL MARK   BILL MARK

ABOVE: Toots steps between two tough gentlemen—Johnny Broderick and Jack Dempsey. BELOW: Toots with a multimillion-dollar-supporting cast: (left to right) Frank Gifford, Eddie Arcaro, Whitey Ford, Charlie Conerley, and Kyle Rote

TOP: Toots smiles through his tears, brandy-flavored, at the "win-or-lose" party given at his place by Frank McMahon (to his right) after McMahon's unbeaten Majestic Prince lost the first race of its life—the Belmont Stakes. Jane Russell takes it in good shape. Considine rechecks the results. CENTER: Toots kibbitzing with a solvent friend—Dave Mahoney, president of Norton-Simon. BELOW: Toots congratulates *Mrs.* Gene Cernan instead of the Apollo 10 astronaut at his back. Others at Shor's choice corner table are Earl Wilson, Broadway columnist, Mrs. Tom Stafford, Astronaut Stafford and, on the right, Bob Considine.

CHAPTER 7

"You're holding the hand of the President of the United States."

TOOTS could use some luck. New Yorkers have short memories. Grand Central Terminal or the Statue of Liberty could go out of action for a couple of years and nobody would know how to find them when they reopened. Toots needed old friends back and new ones to take the places of those who had died and those who had drifted.

What an original cast of characters had surrounded Toots, and vice versa! They left their initials carved on his old bar, their affection etched on his heart and liver, and, in some cases, their books in his curious little library.

Jim Bishop put Toots in fast company in his *Some of My Very Best.*

> Three of the men I admire have little in common. One is Dwight D. Eisenhower; the second is Francis Cardinal Spellman; the third is Toots Shor. A President, a cleric, a restaurateur. A Presbyterian, a Catholic, a Jew. Texas, Massachusetts, Pennsylvania. Soldier, author, "illiterateur."
>
> To my knowledge, he has never been nominated for a brotherhood award. And yet, Shor has done more for brotherhood than anyone I know. Annually, he has collected and donated money for Catholic Charities in New York, more money than 99 per cent of the Catholics. He loves his fellow man and in this he follows the precepts of Christianity, although he will live and die in the great faith of his fathers."

"Toots is unfeigned, crudely frank, quick-witted, generous, ever-thankful for his destiny and a true friend of more

164

name athletes, I expect, than any layman that ever lived," said Fred Russell of the Nashville *Banner,* who inherited the late Grantland Rice's unflagging graciousness, assessed his sometimes less-than-gracious friend in his book *Bury Me in an Old Press Box.*

Earl Wilson inscribed his *Gazing Into My 8-Ball* to Toots as follows: "To Toots, the South Philadelphia intellectual who will need some help reading my big words." Bob Hope's *I Owe Russia $1,200* was autographed, "Dear Toots. Have somebody explain this to you." Stan Musial was helpful. The Baseball Hall of Famer wrote on the flyleaf of his un-indexed book, "Dear Toots: You're on pages 228 and 229." Quentin Reynolds was even more cooperative. In one of his books he wrote, "Dear Tootsie: You only have to read pages 144, 145, 146, 147, 148, 203, 204, 214, 268, 271, 316, 323, and 327. They're the only pages about you."

The authors of some of the books in Toots's library— which is conveniently in the bar of his apartment—wished not to be forgotten as fellow bums. Irving Kupcinet of the Chicago *Sun-Times* wrote, "To Toots, from that crum bum Kup." Bill Veeck, one of the few men Toots ever let in the old place without a necktie, offered in his inscription, "Who else would let a bum like me in? Only a bum like you. Many thanks for many, many things; for your kind-ness, understanding, thoughtfulness, and class." In a first edition of *Timberline,* Gene Fowler scribbled, "To Baby and Toots—America's Sweethearts—from a bum who used to hope to be a gentleman. It's too late now." Fowler signed it "The Sot of Beverly Hills."

Jimmy Durante autographed *Schnozzola,* a biography of him by Gene Fowler, to Toots: "Please don't hang out with me. You'll disgrace me."

Quent Reynolds was the steadiest contributor to Toots's eccentric library. One of his autographed books is espe-cially treasured by Toots. The inscription (apparently done after a long night in Toots's company) reads, "Too bad you can't read this because you are so illeterat" [*sic*]. In his book about Willie Sutton, the fabled bankbuster and jail-breaker, Reynolds wrote: "Dear Toots: Willie asked me to thank you for hiring him when he was on the lam in 1949. He also asked you not to lose the key he gave you to his safety deposit box, containing certain personal belongings he obtained from the Corn Exchange Bank. He will be in touch with you soon, as soon as you send him a cake—as you did once before, just before he sawed his way out." In his *70,000 to One* Quent wrote, "Tootsie, I figured that if people will buy your food they'll buy anything. So I wrote this book." In *Courtroom* he observed, "Toots, you'll find many of your old friends mentioned in this book. Just for luck I had to stick you on page 357. It's the only page in the book you'll read."

The library is not exclusively Toots's. Jimmy Cannon's *Who Struck John* carries this legend: "To Baby and Toots: My foster parents and also my adopted children." Edward Bennett Williams, in the front of his *One Man's Freedom*, penned, "To Baby, the First Lady of New York: the first copy of the first edition. With love, Ed. P.S.—This book tells you what to do until I can get there."

Fowler, personally delivering his biography of Jimmy Walker, *Beau James*, wrote in it, "To Baby and Toots, both of them beautiful in different but important ways. Thanks for giving the great Jim happy Friday nights during his seven last years. A salute! Get in line—I'll kiss both of you. With deep love—Gene."

Toots's 5-Foot Shelf's autographs and tributes also run the gamut all the way from sentiment to sentimentality.

In *Off and Running*, published posthumously with the help of Arthur Mann, Bill Corum wrote a passage that Toots still turns to whenever he wishes to shed tears:

> We had a tough time with him [when he sold 51 West 51]. He had a million dollars for the first time in his life, but you'd have thought from the way he blubbered and threatened to drink all the brandy in stock that Baby had left him and taken the kids.
>
> Actually, I think Toots was overcome by the thought of not having a place to hang out at night with the gang. You may think I'm exaggerating, but that's the way he is and always has been. . . . Our biggest worry was

that he'd find some way to get rid of the money. I know from experience that he's one of the quickest to reach with the ready remedy when a friend is in trouble, and I don't know anybody I've rushed quicker to for help.

We had something of an argument on this score on Thanksgiving Day, 1958, which I spent with Toots and his family in their beautiful home.

I had come out of the hospital pretty sick, but well enough to enjoy a holiday dinner of eggnog. Tootsie insisted that I needed money. I insisted that I needed only appetite and some weight, since I had liberal hospitalization coverage and two good jobs paying me well for doing nothing—though I was writing the column against orders. In fact, I was in a position to lend him a little scratch, if his big check bounced.

We laughed. After so many years of touch and go and of digging down with mutual aid, here we sat, both loaded, with no way to help each other.

The moving passage was in the mood of the inscription Sid Feder wrote in *Murder, Inc.*, which condemned, among others, a friend of Toots's named Lucky Luciano: "To Tootsie—The heart who walks like a man, who is only your best friend when you need one. Always gratefully, Sid."

Pat O'Brien pulled out another affection stop. He dipped his pen in pious sunshine and wrote to his cherished friend: "To my guy Toots. How about joining me in a Trip Down Memory Lane and may the Wind STAY at your Back. Always. God keep His arm around you and Your Precious Brood. Your Pal thru the Years. Pat."

Inside *The Wind at My Back* Pat wrote: "On all of our visits to New York, my first stop off, even before registering at the hotel, was to see a walking bear called Toots Shor. Maybe too much has been written about Toots, but there he is, an Irish-looking Jew, twice life-size, built like a bulldozer, and features to match.

" 'I'm unique,' Toots will modestly tell you, as he puts a ham-sized paw on your shoulder and gives you that craggy smile of friendship. 'I'm a bum's bum.' "

Feeling no pain whatever, Pat and Toots hired a venerable horse-drawn hack one very late and rainy night, in front of the Plaza, and insisted that the damp old Irishman come down off his seat and sit inside. *They'd* drive. They did too. They called on Bill Corum and his mother, who were living at the Park Lane, then clopped up to 480 Park. They hitched the horse and persuaded the unhappy cabbie to come along with them to the elegant Shor apartment for a nightcap. They rolled in, dripping water. "Somebody must have bust a cloud someplace," Toots said, still holding the whip. He called upstairs to wake Baby and have her come down. Baby did. She took one look at the three and said, "*All* of you, get out!" The wonder is that they hadn't asked the horse in.

On another disastrous occasion, Toots and Art Rooney, owner of the Pittsburgh Steelers, looked out on West 51st Street and were surprise to note that it was daylight. Rooney said he had to go to St. Patrick's for Mass; it was Palm Sunday. Toots said, "I'm witcha," so off they went. Rooney led the uncertain procession of two down the center aisle, looking for a couple of seats. Toots followed close behind, casing the joint. Suddenly Rooney saw an empty spot in one of the pews and genuflected. Toots, still casing, went right over him and landed thunderously in the aisle. On the way out, after Mass, Toots took a chunk of palm as big as a baseball bat. It was going to be his "saver" at home because he had forgotten (1) his key and (2) to tell Baby where he had been all night. Baby, about one third his size and weight, answered the door buzzer. "Hello, Husky," Toots said dimpling. "I know you'll be happy to know I been to Mass." The devout Mrs. Shor said, "So I see." She took the bat-sized palm and clouted him over the head with it.

James A. Michener, another famed author-friend Toots doesn't read, went to some pains and probably expense to paste on the frontispiece of his *Rascals in Paradise,* by himself and A. Grove Day, a printed author's note:

> Originally, eleven chapters of this book were submitted to the publisher; but upon advice of counsel and after due consideration of the laws governing public

decency, Chapter XI was suppressed. The Postmaster-General said that if it wasn't, the book would be barred from the mails.

Chapter XI was entitled:

TOOTS SHOR: HORSEMEAT AND HAMBURGER.

It contained episodes revealing items of reprobacy and nonfeasance by the subject as follows: backsliding, sowing of wild oats, Corybantism, overparking, hardness of heart, Sabbatarianism, pantophagy, pudicity, antinomianism, barratry, shooting albatrosses, simony, crapulence, nepotism, robbing Peter to pay Paul, breach of promise, celebrating the witches' Sabbath, iconoclasm, dirty pool, chthonianism, Machiavellianism, Sybaritism, misprison of felony, plagiarism, anthology, and assorted torts.

Since Random House books sometimes find their way into family circles, and since the line of common decency must be drawn somewhere, this chapter has regretfully been destroyed, even though the authors considered it the most rascally and revealing of the entire volume.

Toots hopes to finish it some day. The salutation, that is.

Toots's friend, Ernest Hemingway, is succinctly represented in the bookcase, particularly on the flyleaf of *The Short Stories of Ernest Hemingway.* "Dear Toots: I used to know an old whore, very good friend, who referred to this as Too Many Short Stories by Papa. Ernie." Just before John Bainbridge's fond three-part profile on Toots was printed in *The New Yorker,* Hemingway had been peeled layer by layer in the same magazine by that complete mistress of minutiae, Lillian Ross. He emerged like the nucleus of an onion.

Hemingway compared the two treatments, then wrote Toots a note: "Me they knock and a Philadelphia pimp they boost."

Hemingway autographed his *Across the River and Into the Trees* * with "Dear Tootsie: Please ruffle the pages to let people think you read it."

---

* Toots thought it was a book about golf, according to sports columnist Joe Williams.

A blunt friend who could never understand what Toots had in common with personages in the arts and sciences, on the merry-go-round at 51 West 51, once tried to put his puzzlement in words.

"Toots," he said, "I saw you having a long dialogue tonight with Robert Sherwood. I think he's a genius. What the hell could you have been saying to *him?*"

"I was fading him with grunts," Toots said.

Toots was bound to some well-known patrons by other methods than grunts. The rapport with Hemingway was of a sturdier texture than a grunt. They'd go to the fights together at Madison Square Garden or the Yankee Stadium or the Polo Grounds, come back to the place, drink, and debate the merits and demerits of the gladiators. Occasionally, drunk, Hemingway would want to go looking for a fight or an argument at any cheap bar he could find. Toots, drunk, would go with him to protect him if he got in over his head.

They had gambling in common too, but Toots had taken the pledge by the time Hemingway was beginning to go strong. Toots placed bets for him.

"The last bet Hem made with me he called me from Spain wanting to bet a thousand dollars on Ingemar Johansson against Floyd Patterson, the champion, in 1959. I told him he was crazy, he shouldn't do it. But he did it. I placed the bet for him at four to one and he won four thousand dollars. He came through the country after that and stopped by the joint to pick up the money. He was the only man I knew who bet on Johansson. Nobody figured he had a chance because he didn't know how to duck. . . . Must've been the last time I saw Ernie."

The saloonkeeper and the Nobel Prize winner were closer, let's say, than Hotchner, who wrote *Papa Hemingway,* the first of the mounting biographies of Ernie. "I remember him vaguely," Toots says, somewhat like Clive Barnes reviewing Minsky's. "He went to a couple of World Series games with me and Ernie. Hemingway needed company. He couldn't get around too well. This guy sort of waited on him, hand over foot. He had a tape recorder."

Toots's great admiration for the author of *For Whom the Bell Tolls* never related to his writing style. Indeed, Hemingway once conceded that Toots could write even better; surely write briefer sentences. When Hemingway, having been reported dead in a safari plane crash, emerged triumphantly from an African jungle days later brandishing a bottle of gin and a bunch of bananas, Toots sent him a cable. A one-word cable: "Showboat."

Toots, who occasionally goes on awesome weight-losing diets ("I haven't had a bowl of chili for six weeks, that I can remember") gave Hemingway good marks for a diet he perfected near the end of his life. Hemingway first revealed it to a reporter with whom he was drinking at Shor's bar. The reporter had noticed that Hemingway had lost a lot of weight and asked him how he did it.

"I stopped drinking with creeps," the great man said seriously. "As long as I can remember, I drank with creeps. I'd go into a bar anywhere in the world, somebody would spot me, make a big thing about buying me a drink, and finally I'd say, 'Sure, thanks, and now have one on me.'

"So I'd wind up drinking with this creep I had never seen before and didn't want to be with and never wanted to see again. I took on a lot of booze that way over the years. One day I decided to stop drinking with creeps. I decided to drink only with friends. I've lost thirty pounds as a result."

Pulitzer Prize-winning playwright and FDR's foremost prose polisher, Robert Sherwood, seldom missed Shor's for luncheon whenever in the city. "I'll never forget," Toots says solemnly, "he drank Dubonnet and vodka cocktails. He liked to talk sports, and I think I can talk sports as good as anybody. Sherwood was one of the fine men of our world. He never forgot that I really predicted and really was sincere that Mr. Truman would win in 1948. At lunch he'd talk baseball or whatever was in season, but now and then he'd tell us stories about Mr. Roosevelt, Harry Hopkins, and others he worked with in Washington. Gleason would sit down every once in a while and try to get intellectual with him and spoil the whole conversation.

"One of the great nights we had in the joint was when

Sherwood and Averell Harriman came back to the store after
Harriman had made a speech at the *Herald Tribune* Forum.
We talked about everything except what was tops in their
minds: Harriman was flying the next day to Tokyo to see
MacArthur to give him Truman's message to pipe down—
he wasn't President."

There was little that Sherwood would not do for Toots. At
Toots's request, Sherwood wrote a most touching one-act play
about Ernie Pyle, based on the great war correspondent's
taking leave of the war in Europe and taking off—with grave
premonitions—toward his meeting with a bullet on Ie Shima
in the Pacific. It was Sherwood's contribution to a TV special
that raised $100,000 for the Overseas Press Club of America.
A buddy of Toots was president of the club that year.

Sherwood even played baseball for Toots, a concession that
could be compared to Abraham Lincoln's acceptance of Mary
Todd Lincoln's nagging demand that he frug with her at a
White House cotillion. Toots had put together a ball club
expressly for the purpose of challenging a celebrity team he
heard was being assembled by 21.

"I had Sherwood playing second base and Eddie Arcaro
playing shortstop," he recalls. "We had Jimmy Demaret,
three-time Masters winner; Arcaro, five-time Derby winner;
Don Budge, the first guy to win all four big tennis titles in
one year; Rocky Marciano, Rocky Graziano, Joe Louis, Margaret Truman, and Audrey Meadows as coaches; Bugs Baer
at third: Shipwreck Kelly, Joe DiMaggio and Carl Hubbell
spread around. All in shirts saying 'Toots Shor.' We had a
good time going out to the Polo Grounds in the bus, and a
better time coming back. We beat 21, naturally. The only
class they had was Jinx Falkenberg. Pitching.

"I had one tough decision to make during the game. I took
Sherwood out and moved Shipwreck in at second. Well, we
got back to the joint and we're all stretched out with these
shirts on and Sherwood said to somebody, 'I don't mind,
really, but to be jerked by a jerk is too must to bear.' "

Toots's softball team moved up in class, unfortunately, and
its one-game winning streak ended. This time it challenged
and was put to rout by a team of overage ballplayers and

showfolk managed by Leo Durocher. Most notable play of that game, played at the Yankee Stadium before a moderately patient crowd that had paid to see the regular game to follow, was Toots's swinging bunt off the enemy pitcher—again that long, lean, crafty righthander, Jinx Falkenberg.

Bill Dickey, behind the plate, scooped up the ball as Toots started for first base and threw it into right field. Tommy Henrich fumbled around with it and Toots headed for second. Henrich threw it high over the second baseman's head, and the third baseman let it go through his legs into the dugout. But third was as far as Toots could run, thus depriving himself of probably the first bunted home run in the history of the House That Ruth Built.

Sherwood lunched in Shor's on the last day of his life. "I'll never forget, I cashed a check for one hundred dollars for him," Toots says. "He died that night. It was one of the few times I ever saw DiMaggio cry. Joe had a date to have dinner with Sherwood the following week."

Toots doesn't talk about DiMaggio as much as he once did. And vice versa.

Neither wishes to talk about the frigid cooling off of their once intensely close relationship. They had been inseparable. Toots once flattened a fan at Yankee Stadium for booing DiMag. A mutual friend once saw the great center fielder running down Sixth Avenue one afternoon and asked him what-on-earth. "I just had lunch at 21 and I'm hurrying to Toots's to tell him I did before somebody else does," Joe puffed. "It wasn't my fault. Somebody in the Yankee front office invited me and I couldn't say no."

DiMag's respect for Toots's judgment made Damon and Pythias look like the McCoys and the Hatfields. Frank Graham and Dick Hyman, in their *Baseball Wit and Wisdom*, touched on DiMaggio's awe of Toots. Quoting Toots, they wrote:

> "Joe paid me one of the greatest compliments I ever had. He and Tom Meany were doing a magazine piece and Tom called me one afternoon and said, 'I'm with your friend, DiMag. I just asked him how he would make a certain play....' As I recall it, Toots said, 'It was a

cutoff play.' Anyway, Tom said, 'He told me how he would make it and I told him the way I had learned it from Wilbert Robinson and John McGraw and he said I should call you and ask you how *you* would make it.'

"Can you imagine that? He wouldn't go along with Uncle Robbie or McGraw. He left the decision up to *me!*

"Everybody in baseball had the greatest respect and affection for DiMag. With all the ability he had, they still wanted to help him when, as it happens to all of us, he needed help. One night when Jimmy Dykes was managing the White Sox he was in the joint for dinner. This was just after the third game of a four-game series and Joe hadn't got a hit yet and Jimmy said to me, 'When you see the Dago again, tell him I said he should loosen up. He's lunging at the ball.'

"I called Joe that night and told him what Dykes had said. The next day—boy, did he hit the Sox pitchers! A home run . . . a double . . . two singles! He ruined them!

"That night, on his way to the train, Dykes called me.

" 'You ———!' he said. 'At least you could have waited for me to get out of town!' "

One version of their break was a mix-up over Joe's failure to show up in Annapolis, Maryland, for a testimonial dinner given by a predominantly Italian-American group for Navy football coach Eddie Erdelatz, who was beset by the Academy's director of athletics. Shor's show-of-confidence delegation from New York was to have been made up of DiMag and John Daly. DiMag missed. A number of Italians who had bought tickets to the dinner baited Shor, asking him repeatedly where his great pal was. Aggravated after a time, Shor roared, "Listen, you guys, you've got John Daly. What more do you need? What do you want—blood? To hell with my Dago friend."

This was duly reported to DiMag, and the cool set in.

"We're both stubborn," Toots says today, still missing him. "We helped each other from the time he first came to New York. I kind of brought him out of his shell. He was a very shy guy. Ed Barrow once said to George Weiss, at a Yankee meeting, 'Lucky we got Toots to be with Joe.' He didn't talk much, even to me, especially when there was anybody else around. One night, when he and Lefty Gomez and I were having dinner and Lefty, as usual, was making everybody who came up to the table laugh, and even gabbing with people at other tables, Joe said to me, kind of sadlike, 'I wish I could be like Lefty but I can't and I know people who meet me go away saying to themselves that I'm a swelled-headed Dago.'

"Joe's always very nice to Baby and our kids. As for me, Joe and I speak when our paths cross, which isn't very often. We sat together at the first Washington Baseball Writers dinner, year or so ago. He's the greatest ballplayer we ever had, and one of the two greatest competitors I've ever known. The other was Ben Hogan.

"One night his brother Dom came into the joint after making three hits and robbing Joe of a couple of triples. The Red Sox had won real easy. I called Joe and asked him to join me and Dom for dinner. Joe said, 'Are you nuts? I'm not eating with *him!*'"

Jimmy Walker was a memorable fixture at 51 West 51.

"I met Jim first in a speakeasy, maybe Leone's," Toots says. "Just hello. The first place I sat down with him was at the Casino in the Park when Eddy Duchin was playing there. Walker was a friend of the fellow who ran the Casino, Sid Solomon. So was Jim Farley.

"Eddy was living at the Victoria Hotel on Seventh Avenue and I was living in the St. Moritz on Central Park South. I went to him and said, 'You've got to live in style. Move up to the St. Moritz. It's a better locale for you.' So he moved and I'll never forget: Eddy and I would walk up through Central Park to the Casino and eat on the cuff. I didn't have any dough and he didn't have too much. Solomon wasn't paying him regularly. So we'd eat, and what prices! But all we'd do was sign.

"Then Eddy went on radio—at five o'clock each day—and became society's favorite piano player and orchestra leader. He had more style and class than anybody, any actor or any man. Through Eddy, I got to know Walker a little better.

"I had the Tavern when Jimmy came back from his long stay in Europe. Hellinger brought him in. We got to be closer and when I lost the joint and was knocked out for a couple of years, I'd see him once each week or two for dinner.

"When I opened my first joint we had a picket line. Jimmy at that time was with David Dubinsky and those people in the garment center. He was an arbitrator. He and Dubinsky came up to the place one day and the line was there. Dubinsky said he couldn't walk through it. But Walker said, 'Well, *I* am. This is my friend. I don't think he could do anything wrong.' How about that?

"So Dubinsky came through with him. I sat down and told him my problem. Pretty soon Lou Dubow, who represented the union that was giving me a hard time, started coming in too. But it was Walker who led the way. He was one of the great men of anybody's life."

Toots became a hero worshiper of Walker at a low ebb in the former mayor's life. Walker's political career had been crushed by the Seabury Investigation of Tammany Hall in the late 1920's. He had chosen self-exile in Europe and had alienated the affections of many loyal supporters by divorcing his wife of many years and marrying an attractive younger woman, Betty Compton. But once home again, Toots treated him as he had been treated during his glittering period as the world's most famous mayor. He saw to it that whenever he came into 51 West 51 he had the best table in the room. One night when Walker arrived, Toots said, "Before we start eating, Jim, come on upstairs. I want to show you something." Toots had assembled every well-known fighter he could corral, for a surprise party for the man who—as an assemblyman in Albany—had legalized professional boxing in New York State. The reception caused tears of gratitude.

Another night Toots gave a little dinner for Walker and Joseph V. Connolly, president of King Features Syndicate and a top man in the Hearst empire. Connolly, who admired Walker and had a lot of the former mayor's verve, had placed him on a retainer of five hundred dollars a week and five hundred dollars expenses during Walker's stay abroad. In return, Walker would occasionally send back a wry and witty feature on his observations in the alien corn.

"It was nice of you to send that money every week, Joe," he said.

"Forget it," Connolly said. "We made more than that off your pieces every week."

Toots was grateful for the exchange.

"Whether he did or not, he made Jim believe it," he remembers.

Friday nights were special for Walker during his last years.

"He'd come in the place, sit down and have dinner with Baby and me, Doc Newman, and whoever else we were taking to the fights at the Garden. He'd have his second scrod of the day. He always did on Fridays. He would have had the first one at lunch. We didn't list it on the menu for dinner, but we always set one aside for him to have.

"We'd always come back to the joint after the fights. One night Johnny Broderick, who never wanted me to drink, came back to the joint a little time after we had arrived. We're sitting at a table in the back. The joint is jammed, as it always was after the fights. Jim had ordered a big double bourbon and a glass of milk. He had knocked off the bourbon, quick, and was sipping the milk when Broderick came up to the table. I'm just getting my brandy and Johnny says, 'Why don't you drink what the mayor's drinking—milk? Will you never learn?' And Jimmy's got this big hooker of bourbon in him.

"No man enjoyed a drink more than Jimmy, and no man ever handled it better."

That is Toots's finest accolade to a departed friend and customer.

Toots had other friends who liked him well enough to stay away from his store. Among them were Luciano, Siegel, Zwillman, and Joe Adonis. Frank Costello was less shy.

"I called Zwillman by his right name, Abner or Abe," Toots says in discussing his immense range of friends. "He was one of the finest characters I ever met. He never swore, never raised his voice to his wife or his children. He was the only one of them called up who didn't take the Fifth Amendment before the Kefauver Committee.

"He was only a bootlegger. Shouldn't those who bought

from bootleggers been as much a part of the crime as the bootlegger? I met him in a nightclub near the end of prohibition. He was with Adonis and Benny Siegel, the last of the Jew tough guys. They ought to put up a statue to Benny in Las Vegas. He built the first big hotel and casino along the 'Strip,' the Flamingo. Now Las Vegas is one of the biggest convention towns in the world, and good enough for Howard Hughes to invest in. Benny called me once and asked me to fly out there and see the Flamingo, which was being built for him by Del Webb. I said, 'Why should I? I see the Waldorf-Astoria every day, why should I go all the way to Las Vegas to see your creepy joint?' He laughed. All those guys liked to laugh. Laugh and play horses. They were all suckers for a hot tip."

They were, but sometimes things did not turn out as planned.

During World War II, while visiting his partner in the slot-machine racket, New Orleans' Phil Kastell, Costello received a call to hurry back to New York as quickly as he could. Plane seats were being parceled out on a strict priority basis at the time. Costello turned the job of getting a ticket over to Kastell, who could fix almost anything in that area. Kastell came through with a ticket which he assured Costello was of the highest priority. Gratefully, Frank handed out black-market nylons to Kastell's staff and headed for the airport.

He was bumped off the plane at Atlanta and told that it might be days before there would be a seat available for New York. Kastell had gotten him a lower priority than artificial flowers.

In his rage Costello hatched a remarkable plot to take revenge on his partner. He bought a *Racing Form*, gave it a good scanning, and selected the two worst horses running the next day at Fairgrounds, the New Orleans track. Then he called Kastell, who was not a horse player, and touted him on the two goats.

"Everything's fixed solid," he assured his friend. "Bet real big. They can't miss."

"Where are you calling from," Kastell asked.

"From Toots Shor's in New York," Costello said. "Got here

safe and sound, thanks to you, Phil. Now remember, shoot the works."

When Costello finally reached New York by train a couple of days later, still chuckling over the revenge he had taken, there was a note at his office to call Kastell. When Kastell came to the phone there was a tear in his voice.

"Frank, I'll never be able to thank you enough for those tips," he said. "Imagine, both of them winning and one of them paying eighty dollars. I can't imagine where you came up with them. Everybody down here said they were a couple of mules, but I said my friend wouldn't give me no mule, and I bet a real bundle on both of them. You're a real pal."

"Zwillman was the class of that crowd," Toots says with affection in his voice. "Our two families became friendly when I rented a summer place in Jersey—1944, maybe—and he stuck me in the West Branch Beach Club. We'd play gin around the pool . . . drink . . . kibbitz . . . while our daughters were splashing around in the pool and Baby was gabbing with Mrs. Zwillman, one of the most beautiful women I've ever seen."

In time the Kefauver Committee issued a subpoena for Zwillman to appear. He couldn't be located. (He was fishing off the Jersey coast on the yacht of Moe Dalitz, later one of the owners of Wilbur Clark's Desert Inn at Las Vegas.) So the committee summoned Toots.

"Where's Zwillman?" committee counsel Rudy Halley, a frequent patron at Shor's, asked with his lisp.

"I don't know," Toots said, honestly enough.

"Why have there been so many phone calls between you two?" Halley pressed him.

Toots was pleased with the tough question. It gave him a chance to embark on his favorite subject: friendship. He did at some length. For a clincher, which made pious old Senator Charles W. Tobey wince, Toots related: "When our first daughter was born, a month after Abner's daughter was born, he sent me a wire saying 'I have a weak back too.'"

In a subsequent appearance, televised, Toots was asked if he could confirm or deny a report that had come to the committee to the effect that Owney Madden was "running things in New York" from his redoubt in Hot Springs, Arkansas. Toots let out a massive snort.

"Doesn't that sound silly, Congressman?" he said to the Senator who posed the question. "How could a guy in Arkansas run *us*?"

Asked to appear again, to be questioned about the reported high spending of Costello, including at Shor's, Toots laughed out loud on the witness stand.

"Costello? He's a cheap guy, gentlemen, a real bum tipper, my waiters tell me. My place is not an expensive joint. *You* could afford to eat there."

The committee seemed relieved to dismiss the witness, with thanks.

Zwillman eventually appeared, disarmed the committee by not resorting to the Fifth Amendment, and chided it when several members wanted to know if he had ever met Virginia Hill, the dazzling moll who played the leading feminine role in that first widely televised Congressional hearing. Zwillman looked at his questioners reprovingly and said, in his soft voice, "Gentlemen, why would you ask me a question like that? Don't you realize that my wife is watching this show?"

Zwillman never came near Toots's restaurant during the years when the Kefauver Committee and other arms of government, notably the Internal Revenue Service, had the heat on him. Even harder, he remained away from the wake and funeral of Baby's mother, whom he adored, because he felt his presence might embarrass the family.

Edward Bennett Williams, the Washington attorney, who followed the Zwillman tax cases closely, declared indignantly, "This man is as clean as a whistle." But the constant pressure, the spotlight, and the notoriety began to break him up. On top of everything else, he learned that his daughter had been excluded from a school party or two, and his son was having to fight an occasional classmate berater.

"So he took his life," Toots says. "He did it because he was a great family man. He figured his wife and kids would get a better break in life if he bowed out. How's that for class? Abner was a Jew who worked at his religion, but a monsignor named Dulaney must have prayed a good thirty minutes at the side of the coffin on the night of the wake. Some creep suggested I shouldn't go to the funeral: I'd be photographed and that wouldn't be good for the store. Abner never had a piece of my action; none of those guys did.

"So I went to the funeral, of course. Abner was my friend."

Toots was close to John Kieran too, Clifton Fadiman, Bennett Cerf, Franklin P. Adams, and Dan Golenpaul, the man who put them all together, made "Information Please," and would lead the pack into Shor's place after every show. He listed the delicate Paul Draper among his better friends and vigorously defended the dancer against political charges lodged against him during the McCarthy purges. He even went to Carnegie Hall to see Paul pirouette, and had a jarring setback as he left that hallowed place.

"Toots Shor's," Toots said to the cabdriver as he cascaded into the hack.

The driver seemed startled.

"Mister," he said, pulling away from the curb, "I've been working this stand for ten years and this is the first time I ever took anybody from here to there."

Toots's self-improvement program while at 51 West 51 brought him in contact—sometimes abrasive—with many other patrons of the arts. He even dressed up and went to the Metropolitan to hear *Faust*. There he met Elsa Maxwell, who formed a swift and not very kind appraisal of his credentials.

"You don't seem to know anything about opera, Mr. Shor," she said later on a radio show that incredibly had room for both.

"That makes us even, Miss Maxwell," Toots said cheerfully. "You don't seem to know anything about baseball."

As for *Faust*, Toots dismissed it in three words when he returned to his store: "Too much singing." He was constantly amazed that he hardly knew a soul whenever he ventured into the world of the arts. "There isn't a crum here I know," he said to Rags Ragland the night (never completely understood) when they showed up at Leopold Stokowski's symphony concert. "Let's leave at the half."

People were sometimes startled to see Toots away from

his métier. "What are *you* doing here?" Leonard Lyons exclaimed upon sight of him at a Doubleday party for Elizabeth Janeway. (Toots had been invited by his friend, Jimmy Conzelman, the football coach.)

"Just drinking and being literary," Toots replied.

Sometimes he went alone in search of the cultural life.

"Where you been?" a barfly asked him as he came into his place late one afternoon, looking harried.

"I just took in a movie about a bunch of crazy Russian actors running around and yelling," he explained. "It's called *The Brothers Kalamazoo*."

It was not the first movie Toots viewed through his personal Rosetta stone. His friend Sam Zimbalist of MGM gave him two tickets to the opening of *Quo Vadis* because he wanted Toots to see the performance of Buddy Baer, Max's massive young brother and sometime boxer, who had a part in the picture. It was the Circus Maximus scene in which the virginal heroine was tied to a stake, a maddened bull released in the expectation of goring her to death, and a giant loinclothed slave—Buddy—set out to protect her with his bare hands. There was a terrifying close-up of the bull charging the cringing virgin, then a close shot of Buddy Baer hurtling in front of the bull, and a still closer shot of Buddy seizing the horns of a bull, another bull. This one started to leak sawdust as Buddy, muscles a'rippling, slowly and agonizingly twisted its neck.

In time the sound track gave off a loud snap and Buddy and the virgin relaxed.

Toots was still perspiring from the ordeal when he returned to the restaurant and found Zimbalist dining there. He brought up the bull-and-Baer scene.

"You liked Buddy in it, eh?" Zimbalist said, pleased.

"Yeah," Toots said. "But it just goes to show you how great Joe Louis really was."

Zimbalist raised a delicate eyebrow.

"Joe Louis?"

"Yeah, he flattened that bum twice."

Mike Todd presented Maurice Evans in *Hamlet* during the height of Toots's culture kick and invited him and Baby to the fancy opening-night performance. Toots joined in the small talk in the lobby during intermission. When the buzzer called the Bard's buffs back into the theater, Toots said, "I bet I'm the only bum in the joint that's going back just to see how it turns out."

The place at 51 West 51 served as a launching pad for Toots's two flights into the rarefied realm of the White House.

"I got a phone call from Bob Hannegan. He told me President Roosevelt was having a tea the next day and he'd like to have me and Baby come to it. I was sitting in the place with Rags and Frank Sinatra having dinner when the call came through. Naturally, I was excited. I picked up the phone and called Baby.

"At that time our daughter Bari was just about a year old. Baby said she had taken sick with a cold and all. I said 'Jiminy crickets, Husky, this is the President of the United States who wants us.' Baby said, 'So I'm going to stay with the baby.' I could tell she meant it.

"Well, now I felt like a guy stuck with two tickets in his pocket. So I picked up the phone and called Hannegan in Washington and told him, 'Baby can't go, but I'm sitting here with Rags Ragland and Frank Sinatra. Can I bring them along?'

"Hannegan said, 'I'll call you back in ten minutes.' I guess he had to check it with Marvin McIntyre or somebody like that. Ten minutes later he called back and said 'Okay.'

"The next afternoon, there we were. The President was sitting there and we all went along in a line to meet him. He was very nice to me, so I knocked the White House food. When Frank was introduced to him he looked at Frank, skinny as a rail, turned his head and said, 'Mac,' to McIntyre, 'imagine this guy making them swoon. He wouldn't have made them swoon in our day, right?' "

Shortly thereafter FDR received a letter from former ambassador to Germany James W. Gerard, longtime fund-raiser for the Democratic party. It read, "I see where you were visited by Frank Sinatra and Toots—male or female? Why don't you get Sinatra to sing for one of our fund-raising din-

ners? It would help us get some money in the party. Toots—
male or female—could be the cashier."

The President replied, in passing, "If you ever saw Toots,
you'd know what he was."

Toots *and* Baby made the last state dinner given in the
White House before the Trumans moved across the street to
Blair House and the work of reconditioning the Executive
Mansion began. Once more the invitation came by way of
Hannegan, by now Postmaster General and godfather to
Kerry Shor.

"White tie, Tootsie," Hannegan said over the phone.

"I look better in a black," Toots said.

"White tie!"

It was a command.

"I went out and got a set of tails made," Toots says when
reliving the adventure. "I'll never forget. Cost me three hundred. I bought a high silk hat too."

Toots wanted very much to be photographed in his splen-
did armor, chiefly to have some fun with the regulars around
his place. A secondary reason was that he was sure he'd never
wear the suit again. All went well, up to a point. Handsome
Labor Department official Jim Reynolds, Quent's younger
brother (who had helped Toots into his livery), escorted
the radiant Baby up the steps under the portico and led her
toward the main doors of the great house. Toots was just
behind them. The photographers closed in on him.

"When I saw them I knew I didn't want a picture," he said
later. "I figured that if Mr. Truman was nice enough to invite
me I didn't want to see them embarrass him by taking the
picture of me and calling me 'saloonkeeper of the week,' or
whatever they wanted. So I growled. 'Take my picture and
I'll break your cameras,' I told them. I was steaming. 'Listen,
I've always tried to do everything I could for you fellows,
but I don't think this is fair. Why me?'"

They held their fire, and the self-censorship deprived future generations of just what Toots looked like at his hour
of triumph.

"I'll never forget," Toots will say. "With all my luck, they
had an opera singer after dinner. I was hoping for a comedian

at least, but Margaret was hooked on opera. But it didn't matter. There I was in the same room with Truman. How a man grows when he becomes President! I'd known Mr. Truman when he was a Senator, then when he was Vice President. He had been in my store a number of times. Now there he was—President.

"After dinner the men went into one room to have a cordial and the ladies went into another room to have a cordial too, I guess. What a thrill it was to see Senator Vandenberg and Senator Taft and all those big shots standing around talking to Mr. Truman—and to see that Mr. Truman was the boss.

"Leaving, we all shook his hand. I wanted to hold it for an extra second or two. You're holding the hand of the President of the United States, I kept thinking. You're holding the hand of the President of the United States!

"It was hard for me to let go."

Harry Truman had come a long way from Independence, Missouri.

Toots had come an even longer way from 15th and Wharton.

CHAPTER 8

"Dear God, here we go again."

IT was like old times when Toots walked up to the doors of his bigger and, hopefully, better place. The same weepy and whiskered bum who had waited for him each working day on the pavement in front of the old place was now there at 33 West 52. Toots didn't ask him how he had survived the two and a half years of Toots's inaction. He handed him a deuce. The bum looked indignant.

"I expected at least a fin," he said. So Toots gave him five dollars. That was December 27, 1961. It is a mark of the loyalty that Toots inspires that the bum hasn't missed a day since.

"He was a good spender when he used to come into Leon and Eddie's when I worked there," Toots says, acquitting the perennial leech.

There were many other linkages to the past: the round bar which all were obliged to pass, though few did, going into or out of the main dining room; the familiar mannish wood paneling and old red brick; a larger and somehow even false fireplace in the rear of the dining room; Ziggy and other bartender-confessors behind the "roulette wheel," as Toots called his booze trough; and a menu that differed from the old only in the matter of updated prices. It was a sign of the times that the sirloin steak Toots charged $2.00 for in 1940 now commanded $7.50. "And I'm going to blow dough on it," he said prophetically.

Chief Justice Warren dropped in to wish him well and have a drink and dinner. Jackie Gleason sent a huge gangster's funeral floral horseshoe. Gleason dictated the message on the card from his pleasure dome in Miami:

Good Luck, Dear Toots,
On Your New Domain,
Where Joy Will Reign
As Well as Tomain.

The floral piece was accompanied by six Care packages.
Gleason refused to pay the florist's bill on the ground that he
had misspelled ptomaine.

"Spelling it wrong spoiled all the fun," Gleason said later.
"Toots pronounced it correctly."

The press was affectionate, as ever.

Jimmy Cannon wrote, in the *Journal-American:*

The new joint is a beautiful saloon. It stands on the
same plot of ground on West 52nd Street where I originally met Toots when he was the day shift manager of
Leon and Eddie's. It took him 29 years to get back where
he started from and there have been a lot of laughs and
some grief along the way.

It was a sort of homecoming for me. Much of my life
has been spent in the places Toots ran and, when he was
out of action, it became a lonelier town. The world
changed but Toots held on to what he was and yesterday
once again he was trudging across a saloon of his own
in that wallowing gait to the laughter of his friends. It is
the only music he appreciates.

He is a tavern keeper in the old tradition. The strays
of the night find their way to his bars, and so do the guys
who make it big. Any place where Toots is has been a
joint where men come to brag when they're proud and
to fight the sorrow when it's bad. This, I imagine, will be
like the others.

Earl Wilson cupped an ear to the sound of laughter:

Groucho Marx was shaking hands with Yogi Berra,
Robert Morse was yelling at Whitey Ford how great it is
to be a father, Walter Cronkite was saying to my B. W.,
"Now you have my new address. Here."

Toots hadn't sent out one invitation, but it was so
crowded it took me two visits to get a drink—the bar was
only nine deep. Groucho, beholding Jack Dempsey and

Rocky Marciano warmly shaking hands, suggested, "The least they could do is go three rounds for us." Hugh O'Brian, rushing over from "First Love," said, "We had 20 people standing tonight!" Groucho said, "Anybody sitting?"

There were astonishingly varied estimates of the price tag of the new place in the assorted accolades. No sports columnist dared soar above $2.5 million. But then there was Donald I. Rogers, financial editor of the *Herald Tribune,* in his new Wall Street prose:

> After an absence of two-and-a-half years, the business community's official midtown luncheon club will reopen tomorrow with no especial fanfare or other kind of respectable observance. . . .
>
> Affable, amiable, gross and sometimes grotesque, but always lovable and loved, Toots Shor has opened himself a new gin mill and eatery . . . with money borrowed from the Teamsters' Union Pension Fund. He has built what is said to be the finest-equipped restaurant in the city.
>
> It cost more than $7,500,000, it is said, and while it generally duplicates his old place, the backstage appointments such as kitchens, freezers, humidors, cooling rooms and such are declared to be unparalleled. Be that as it may, for Shor never attracted the gourmets anyway.

Gourmets to one side, there was no question about the new place's bigness. Toots's first restaurant was paid off completely within a year and a half of its opening, with roast beef at $1.40 and drinks at 50 and 60 cents. There were days there when he grossed $2,000, as opposed to the biggest day the Tavern had had in its prime, $1,100. But it was clear to everybody concerned, with the possible exception of Toots, that it would cost sums of that type just to slip a key in the service entrance of 33 West 52.

No man knew better than Bob Broderick the size of the bite Toots had taken and would now attempt to swallow. Broderick was hired by Toots as a waiter during the Tavern days. He has remained in Toots's eclipsing shadow ever since, disdaining many attractive offers from more stable publicans. His devotion to Toots for more than a third of a century has become a legend in the trade, but many of Toots's regular customers hardly know him. Broderick, now the restaurant's general manager, stays "in the back." It is there that a restaurant's fate is decided.

The tough, competent, little (by comparison to Toots) Broderick looked over the working section of the new Shor's and knew instinctively that it was going to be a battle, the biggest battle of Toots's life. To make the machine run, Toots needed a head day chef and his assistants, a head night chef and his acolytes, a maître d'hôtel, fourteen headwaiters and captains, seventy-eight waiters and busboys, twelve barmen, four butchers, eleven salad men, twenty-six dishwashers, a corps of hat-check girls, more assistance and office equipment for chief accountant Dick Sherman, more cashiers, squads of maintenance men and porters, and sundry others never seen by the jolly people out front.

The "nut" or overhead would be therefore awesome, as would the consumption of goods at the bars and tables on the three floors. This averaged six hundred to eight hundred luncheons and three hundred to five hundred dinners served daily, plus the special parties that would be booked.

"He puts his two cents in," Broderick told interviewer Jean Bennett in an estimate of his idol, "but on the whole he leaves it up to me. And since Toots won't ever fire anybody, that's up to me too."

Toots's food-and-drink bills soon reached $125,000 a month, almost as much as the entire cost of his first restaurant. But he was determined that everything be just the same. He'd suffer and growl when any old friend suggested otherwise.

"I don't like this new bar," a fellow drinker of long standing, and sometimes falling, said to him.

"What's wrong with it?" Toots demanded.

The man shook his head. "It's hard to explain, Toots," he said. "I don't like the new set of drunks you get."

Toots's hardy bevy of lady customers, who range from

Olympic discus throwers to debutantes and from stripteasers to nuns, were not entirely pleased with the new place. They liked the new ground-floor location of the powder room—the idea of an unsung architect named Baby Shor—but the lighting in the main room made them look as if they had been run through a strong bleach.

They said so, shaking him. "I don't remember any of those broads beefing about the lighting in the old joint," he told a friend. He was in no mind to capitulate.

"Men come first," he told a group of ladies from the New York papers he invited to inspect the place. "This is a saloon."

Jimmy Cannon, who swears Toots uses Khrushchev's old tailor, had a complaint about the food.

"You've been eating in them lousy French joints since I got knocked out, so no wonder it's hard to get used to good American food again," Toots said. But Cannon was unimpressed. He began to believe the chef had a personal grudge against him. He pictured him as a large fierce fellow who had trained under the Borgias, and dismissed Toots's loud assertion that there were actually twenty cooks in the kitchen, counting masters and apprentices. Late one afternoon in the joint Cannon was knocking the food. Toots was ignoring him. He was telling another writer that he had finally surrendered to the girls' wishes about more subdued lighting and had just put in an expensive device that would automatically lower the overhead candelabra at precisely 4 P.M. Cannon, continuing his monologue about the food, was paying no attention to what Toots was talking about.

Suddenly, right on the nose of four o'clock, the lights dimmed.

"Thank God they electrocuted the chef!" Cannon cried.

Other friends figuratively dropped hints in Toots's nonexistent Suggestions Box. One was his architect Charles Luckman, whose Lever Brothers glass-and-metal office building on Park Avenue had ignited a trend that lifted the face of Manhattan.

"When we were designing the interiors of the mezzanine men's club—which in itself was a departure for Toots—I was able, after some considerable effort, to persuade him to put up the bronze murals which now grace the walls," Luckman later wrote to a mutual friend.

"Encouraged by this, I took another step which didn't work. I had our top creative people tour all the fine galleries of Manhattan to gather a collection of prints which we felt appropriate for the main dining room of the restaurant. After much work, great expense (our own), special insurance, special guards, and so forth, the pictures were hung in the main dining room late one Friday evening.

"Toots came into the restaurant on Saturday morning about eleven o'clock, took one look, and yelled, 'Take those goddamned art things out of this saloon!' "

Hellinger, Corum, Granny Rice—so many others—had gone. But the faces of many of those who came into 33 West 52 were unchanged, save for two and a half years of additional wrinkles. And the dialogue was generally as provocative.

"How do you like it in Kansas City?" Cardinal Spellman asked tough and peppery Billy Martin at an upstairs charity luncheon to which His Eminence had been invited by his friend Mickey Mantle. Martin had recently been traded by the Yankees.

"Fine, Your Eminence," Billy said, kissing the cardinal's ring. Billy walked a few steps away, then turned to Toots and said indignantly, "How would *he* like it in Kansas City?"

Joseph P. Kennedy, who preferred La Caravelle, dropped by Toots's for lunch not long before he suffered his stroke. Customers at nearby tables were surprised to see the father of the President go into what appeared to be a red-necked rage as he ordered his food and began talking to Toots. On several occasions he rattled the tableware by pounding his clenched fist on the table. He left as abruptly as he had entered.

"What was he sore at you for?" someone asked Toots.

Toots was surprised. "He wasn't sore at me," he said. "He was just telling me how much he likes Bobby. He said Bobby is just like him; would track down and get even with an enemy no matter if he had to go all the way around to find him."

As in the old store, Topic A in the new place frequently had to do with drinking. When Jack Dempsey once took a two and a half year layoff, he lost his heavyweight title. Toots was out of action for a similar length of time but came back drinking strong as ever. The difference in this aimless parallel is that Dempsey didn't practice his art during his time off, and Toots never stopped. But, like Alexander the Great, he was inclined to weep late at night because he had no more opponents to conquer. They were either dead or, like Gleason, had taken to drinking red wine with ice and a Tab as a chaser. Another dear friend who used to go the distance with him had taken the pledge during Toots's interregnum but consented to have a drink with Toots to celebrate the opening. He ordered a Dubonnet on the rocks. A waiter who had known him from the old days looked shocked as he took the order.

"Dubonnet on the rocks?" he asked incredulously. "That's like putting a Band-Aid on a leper."

Toots took up where he had left off—which was the night before he opened. Most often it was brandy-and-soda on the rocks. Like a chain smoker who uses only one match a day, the one he uses to light the day's first cigarette, Toots found a way to eliminate the energy-consuming effort of saying, "I'll have another brandy-and-soda." He'd simply catch a passing waiter's eye and tap the top of his empty glass. Then he'd make a little circle with his forefinger, which meant "Bring another round for everybody."

Some of his older friends had hoped that Toots would begin tapering off, now that he was sixty and beginning by far the most ambitious business undertaking of his life. One day Toots's longtime friend Curly Harris received a somewhat mysterious phone call from Bill McCormack, a politically powerful millionaire who seldom missed having his business luncheons in Shor's. Curly had worked on special assignments for McCormack since his days as a hip Broadway and crime reporter. He sensed from the tone of McCormack's summons that this would be something important.

Curly was ushered into McCormack's office and the door was closed behind him.

"Curly," he said, "what can you do about Toots's drinking?"

After recovering, Harris burst out laughing. All that secrecy, and then *this*. But McCormack saw nothing humorous about his question.

"I'm serious," he snapped. "I want you to go back to Toots right now and tell him that if he stops drinking, I'll give a check for one million dollars to charity."

Curly went back to the place and found Toots where he had left him, at the bar. The proprietor listened attentively to the extraordinary proposition.

"Jiminy crickets, a million bucks," he wheezed. "Go back and tell him I'll stop, never take another drink. All I ask in return is that he give the million to me, not to charity."

Toots by then had become the Oracle of drinking. He might have half a dozen brandies-and-sodas but raise a questioning eyebrow if a newcomer to his table ordered a martini. He calls a martini a "bomb," and is as afraid of them as he is of, say, Baby. "We'll take two bombs and then eat right away," he once said to Frank Conniff, one of the country's leading authorities on the martini. Six bombs later Conniff was in the middle of Wellington's strategy at Waterloo and Toots's head was slowly sinking toward his untouched oxtail soup. Martinis and Toots have never mixed.

Toots starts off each lunchtime by filling in old friends on what sort of a night he had the night before. One day a friend came in for lunch, bringing along a film maker who for some improbable reason had never met Toots. He acknowledged the introduction to the film fellow with a bleak nod and then, turning to his friend with pained merriment in his red-white-and-blue eyes said, "I've been drinking." Before the friend could say, "Well, then, move over," the film maker asked Toots a cheerful but unnerving question.

"What are you celebrating?" he inquired.

Toots and his friend were thunderstruck. It had never occurred to either of them that drinking had anything to do with special occasions. It was just an everyday thing. Like breathing.

The prodigal's return to action did not go unnoticed by the community of which he had become so deeply a part. Though he didn't open his joint until the last week of 1961, Toots was named "Restaurateur of the Year" by the Beer, Wine, and Liquor Industries. He received his "Edgar" at a luncheon at the Waldorf-Astoria in April, 1962, and made a talk. His subject was friendship. It seemed like safe ground to Toots, instead of the material which had been written for him—on demand—by his literary friends. Perhaps he was bewildered by the citation on his "Edgar." It had been outlined to him earlier in a letter from Ed Gibbs, editor of the Industries' *Newsletter:*

"The 'Edgar,'" Gibbs explained to Toots, "is a pride of *achievement* award and judging is on *effectiveness.* That is why we are proud too because it is a credit to this industry to have constructive business men like you representing this great business, a business which is so vital to the American public.

"Please accept our sincere congratulations and—KEEP UP THE GOOD WORK IN 1962!"

Toots figured he had been keeping up the good work too long to be reminded to continue it. What other saloonkeeper in town had buried more friends, loaned more money whether he had it or not, helped his kids with their homework, cowed Aristotle Onassis—who was serving as a judge—into choosing him and Baby as winners of the Sunday Night Dance Contest at El Morocco, showed up at the Father-Daughter dances at Marymount and not only danced with his beautiful daughters but managed to swallow a sip of the nuns' punchless punch?

Who else could say at 4 A.M., closing up the joint with John Wayne, *"We're* going to Kerry's Confirmation at Marymount tomorrow"? Who else could just sit at a table in his place, talking sports, while a thief, a cop, and the lady whose bag had been snatched, plunged into the place? Who else could have continued to talk sports as the cop backed the thief against a wall near the entrance to the kitchen and—much more nervous than the thief—brandished his pistol at the poor man? Who else could have said to the representative of righteousness, the cop, "Watch it, junior; don't come busting in here with a gun," and to the lady, "Listen, sweetheart, next time some guy gives you a heist don't chase him in here, see?"

Who indeed—God bless this man!—would pay $360 for a table at a dinner in his own honor at the Lambs Club? However strange it seemed to his guests, Toots regarded it as a bargain in the long run. After all, Joe E. Lewis, asleep while another of Toots's guests, Dempsey, was delivering a eulogy to Shor, woke up, looked up dazedly at the Manassa Mauler and croaked, "Sit down, ya big fag!" And, for extras, Jack Waldron, the master of ceremonies for the expensive evening, said, "Folks, our door prize is fifty Lawrence Welk records— and a hammer."

Who, indeed, would have guts enough or be dumb enough to get up on the Lambs stage and sing? With many references to script, Toots croaked through an atrocious libretto which went as follows:

MR. WONDERFUL

(When Toots is finally introduced at the end he acknowledges the principal speakers on the dais, then asks for an arpeggio—which ought to get a laugh. Then he goes into the lyric which MUST BE DONE VERY, VERY SLOWLY and, most important, WAIT FOR ALL LAUGHS!

CHORUS
(Very, very slowly)

May I state—it's been great
  And the kind of evening few people rate
But I must confess in all modesty
  Mr. Wonderful—that's me!

There are those—I suppose
  Who'd get hammy if they heard such ku-dos
But I say again in all honesty
  Mr. Wonderful—that's me!

This week you honored Stengel
   One of my great chums
Which only proves this week
   They must be honoring crums.

To you all—in this fine hall—
   Thanks for making this a night to recall
You have treated me most elegantly
   You've been wonderful, simply wonderful
More than wonderful to me!

There wasn't a dry eye in the house, or in Toots's accounting office after the Lambs sent him his bill.

He was done better by in May, 1963, when he received President Kennedy's People-to-People sports award at the Americana Hotel. Bob Hope flew in from California to speak. As he marched to the dais with Toots and the others at the head table, Hope looked over the room. "I've seen more people than this at a *briss*," he said. Later, in tribute to his friend, who was by this time toasting himself, Hope said, "As Secretary of State, Toots could have saved us a fortune. We wouldn't have any allies left to lend to. . . . He has the integrity of Bernard Baruch, the nerve of astronaut Gordon Cooper, the charm of Sonny Liston, and the humility of Milton Berle. . . . He'll give you the shirt off his back, which is great if you want to open a circus. . . . He likes almost everybody. He doesn't care whether you're rich or poor, as long as you're famous."

Frank Sinatra commissioned Sammy Cahn and Jimmy Van Heusen to write a song about Toots to the melody of "That's Why the Lady Is a Tramp." He hired an accompanist. But, after all that, his plane was grounded. All agreed that it may have been the finest song Sinatra never sang:

There's no one like him, nobody at all
   He's twice as wide as Wilt Chamberlin's tall
And is his mouth big? It's just wall to wall
   That's why the gentleman is a champ!

He'll break your back with that ham of a paw
   Then grin a grin like a mother-in-law

Then yell a phrase which would spin Bernard Shaw
  That's why the gentleman is a champ!

He loves those free—fresh—write-ups he gets
  For liquor debts! Big Tough! Big Bluff!

He'd grab your tab, but his arm gets a cramp
  That's why the gentleman is a champ!

He's never learned how to quite say hors d'oeuvres
  But he sure knows about sliders and curves
And does he drink? He drinks more than he serves
  That's why the gentleman is a champ!

His intellect wasn't Harvard designed
  You call him dumb and you're being real kind
Compared to him Yogi Berra has mind
  That's why the gentleman is a champ!

There's no one like him—He will agree
  He adores—he! Big Shor! Big Bore!

Too bad his mouth's not equipped with a clamp
  That's why the gentleman is a champ!

He came from Philly in nineteen oh three
  Worked as a bouncer and made history
Bouncing old ladies was his specialty
  That's why the gentleman is a champ!

He's got a shape like the rear of a barge
  He got that big 'cause he eats free of charge
The food is better in Hoffa's garage
  That's why the gentleman is a champ!

All all you Gentiles I've news for you
  The bum's a Jew. No goy! Oh joy!

With charms like his, he should give a green stamp
  That's why the gentleman
That's why the gentleman
  That's why the gentleman is a champ!

Sinatra planned to finish, to the tune of "But Beautiful"—

> But I'm certain you have guessed
>   The above was all in jest
> As a chum he's passed the test
>   But beau-tee-ful!
>
> If you know the man at all
>   I'm certain you'll agree
> He is everything that Gleason hopes to be.
>
> Every great man needs a guide
>   So there's Baby at his side
> And tonight she's like a bride
>   But beau-tee-ful!
>
> Here's a toast to him for all of us
>   Who had the guts to show
> He's beautiful!
>   But beautiful!
> To know!

Toots, it was said, had spent all afternoon in makeup, having a lump put in his throat. If so, it had to make room for the one that swelled naturally as he listened to the gruffly tender tributes of Pat O'Brien, John Daly, and others. Awash with bathos and brandy, Toots advanced to the microphones for the climactic speech of the night. He gripped the sides of the lectern as if he were choking it and had himself a short, comforting cry. A dozen or so of his literary chums who had worked for a week on his speech leaned forward in their chairs, giving him the "body English" to get started. When he finally did, they wished he hadn't. Toots began reading his script as if it were the first time he ever saw it, which probably was true. To his apparent surprise he heard himself saying, in effect, that he'd rather see Whitey Ford or Charley Conerly lift an arm to throw a baseball or a football than see Leonard Bernstein lift an arm to lead a symphony.

("This fearless declaration of the saloon savant," Earl Wilson wrote the next day in the New York *Post*, "will doubtless go down in history. Just how far down can't be predicted, but it could be pretty far.")

Toots bumbled on in the detached oratorical style of, say, Dwight Eisenhower, to the effect he thought Grover Cleveland Alexander was a bigger guy than Alexander the Great; that he'd rather see Mickey Mantle belt a home run than see the "Mona Lisa"; and that he'd rather understand Casey Stengel than the Einstein theory.

Shelving the script, Toots looked the room in the eye and said, "Any guys doesn't like it, there's something wrong with him!" For a moment it looked like a fight might fill the void left by Sinatra's grounding.

Then, incredibly, Toots launched into a thundering attack on the British!

Later, when the action adjourned to Shor's bar, a drinking Anglophile proposed an explanation for Toots's curious aberration.

"Toots really got his Irish up tonight," he said.

Sinatra finally made it to New York shortly after Toots's big night and left more of a mark on his friend than the song would have. They were doing a little drinking in a neutral territory bar named Jilly's one night when Sinatra clapped Toots on the back to emphasize a point. Toots fell off the stool and broke his wrist. Tremors of the crash at Jilly's were felt in Miami. Gleason skidded and broke *his* wrist.

The two soon posed, showing their plaster casts. It seemed like good publicity to Toots until he received a note from Kerry, by then in Bradford Junior College, saying "Gleason broke *his* arm while working on his television show. But the stories say you fell off a barstool! That doesn't sound so good to the other students."

Toots was getting brittle, but his comeback prowess was as great as his recoveries from bad days and worse nights. Wrist mended, Toots carried off with great skill and decorum an assignment that made him the envy of every restaurateur in New York: the task of feeding and watering the platoon of foreign and domestic cardinals who accompanied Pope Paul VI during his historic day-long visit to New York in the fall of 1965. Cardinal Spellman himself selected Shor as their

caterer. With the help of Bob Broderick, Broderick's assistant
Jack Barry, the noblest Irishman who enters the joint each
day, and maître de Sam Klein, who has worshiped Shor since
he went to work for him in 1941, Toots spread a magnificent
buffet for the Princes of the Church at the archdiocesan
headquarters on Madison Avenue. He serviced it with a carefully selected group of eleven captains and waiters who,
among them, spoke twenty-eight languages. All appeared in
dinner jackets and white gloves.

Toots was unhappy about one thing that day he rubbed
shoulders with some of the most distinguished figures in the
College of Cardinals. He did not have time to order special
service plates for the great occasion. Thus he was forced to
use his regular plates which are of brick red inscribed with
an interwoven T and S. The blending of the initials can easily
be mistaken for S and T. Indeed, when Sonja Henie married
Dan Topping and became Sonja Topping she put the arm on
Toots for an entire service of china- and glassware, thus
saving herself the time and cost of personally monogrammed
ware. Now, on the day of the Pope's visit, Toots arranged for
little round doilies to be placed on the service plates to cover
the insignia of his saloon. Alas, when an old Italian cardinal
raised his cup of soup from his plate the doily stuck to the
bottom of the cup and came up with it, revealing the incrimi-
nating initials. The cardinal studied them quizzically.

"What does this mean?" he asked gently.

One of Toots's waiters, hovering nearby, raised his eyes
piously and said, "It stands for Saint Theresa."

Toots broke a leg not too long after that and some of his
friends hinted darkly that retribution and perhaps even Saint
Theresa might be involved. It happened in his room at the
Statler Hilton in Washington while he was packing to return
home from the Gridiron Dinner where he had been a stick-
out in his white tie and tails, browsing among the best-known
figures in politics, diplomacy, industry, business, and pub-
lishing. The cause of his fall became a long-drawn-out legal
case. But that was not envisioned or would it have been of
any real concern on the night Toots fell. The Man, as the devoted Sam Klein calls him, was badly hurt. The break was a

massive one and high on the fibula. He was in excruciating pain on the way to Georgetown University Hospital.

The friend who went with him in the ambulance said, "Toot's, it's Sunday, and this town's dry, but I'll get you a drink somehow. What do you want?"

Toots made an astonishing answer.

"A Coke," he said.

For the next nine months he did not have a hard drink, an unprecedented dry spell. For the first several months of that period he lay in what amounted to state, at Georgetown. His hospital room became the finest salon and readiest saloon in the city. Chief Justice Warren and other members of the Supreme Court dropped by. So did the future Secretary of State, William P. Rogers, J. Edgar Hoover, Senator Robert Kennedy, Postmaster General Larry O'Brien, Bob and Dolores Hope, Jerry Colonna, Vice President Hubert Humphrey, Senator Stuart Symington, Senator Eugene McCarthy, Joe E. Lewis, Edward Bennett Williams, Robert Kintner, John Daly, Bill Conn, Walter Cronkite, troops of ballplayers, Paul Porter, the Washington sportswriters, itinerant New York columnists, and the like. President Johnson, after conferring with his Undersecretary of Labor James Reynolds at the White House, asked Jim where he was going. Jim said, "Georgetown, to see Toots." Johnson asked him to take along two pictures Toots treasures, one of Lady Bird with the President and one of the President alone. Chief Justice Warren sent Toots half of his seventy-fifth birthday anniversary cake. It was costly, what with the bar going night and day, but it was a triumph socially. For a spell there, a relatively visitorless fellow patient at Georgetown would wheel to Toots's room to join in the action, a hepatitis victim named Clark Clifford.

Toots was confined to a wheelchair after his return to New York. He rode it through his restaurant by day and night, between visits downtown to Dr. Howard Rusk's rehabilitation center. He rose from his wheel in time, graduated to crutches, then a cane, then no visible means of support. Then, on a given day, the word spread that he would partake of a brandy-and-soda. *Newsweek* covered, ABC-TV wheeled in a camera. What with retakes, Toots drank a fifth.

Toots's good friend Herbert Bayard Swope referred to newspapering as the "curse of everydayness." But Toots's whole approach to his job has been the reverse: the "joy of everydayness." When he rolls into a cab in front of 480 Park each morning and says "Toots Shor's" to the driver—who never asks the address—he embarks on an expedition that would kill a guardsman (and his horse). But this day will be unique, he tells himself. It is going to be a better day than that which preceded it, no matter what news Dick Sherman will have for him when he arrives at the place: perhaps the word of another breathtaking tax bill inexorably due, though he is still bleeding from the bill he miraculously managed to pay only last week.

Going to work, Toots is a big game-legged Don Quixote confident that that's a light he sees, " 'way down there at the end of the tunnel." He's got a meeting with "some guys" who are going to make straight his path, level all hills that rise before him. Jiminy crickets, the Man up There—Whatta-ManGod—is in the corner of decency, isn't He? As the cab tools down Park, Toots looks out on the greatest city in the world bar none. He helped make it great; endowed at least a portion of it with his own patented robust style. Years before he had paid it as fine a compliment as it ever received. He had listened patiently to his friend Tom Coleman, Republican National Committeeman from Madison, Wisconsin, extol the merit of steaks in his home town. Coleman concluded his parochial remarks by stating, "Toooots, you can cut them with a butter knife, and when you go to bed that night you go to sleep with the satisfaction of knowing that you've had the best steak in the world." Toots gave this polite consideration, then said, "And when you wake up in the morning you're still in Madison, Wisconsin."

The whiskery bum is waiting for him as he rolls out of the cab in front of 33 W. 52. Toots has the money ready, hands it to him, and lets himself in the door to the left of the locked revolving doors. The revolving doors were the scene of one memorable exit and a startling entrance. One night Red Skelton, who hasn't had a drink for many years, staggered out with his hat turned around, coat half off, necktie askew, and knees knocking. A friend, passing by, tried to support him. "I'm okay," Red whispered to him, "I didn't want to walk out sober and give Toots's joint a bad name." As for the unusual entrance through the doors, some bum, having been told to leave and never come back, went next door to Toots's garage, got into his car, drove it up over the curb, and rammed the revolving door with a splintering crash.

Now, on Toots's average workday, all is quiet as he limps in, ignoring as usual his doctors' stern orders to use his cane. The customers will not be arriving for a couple of hours. A bartender, smoking an after-breakfast cigarette, is putting out the bottled wares that will soon be casting their spell over brokers, news-media people, athletes, coaches, managers, lawyers, advertising executives, public relations men, actors, merchants, dealers, wheelers, FBI agents, and of course, Toots. Sam Klein is there at his post, mulling over the luncheon reservations. Broderick and Jack Barry are somewhere "in the back." But Sherman's the man Toots wants to see. They go by elevator to Toots's office on the mezzanine, pass through the outer office that is guarded by Grace Nielsen, the secretary who has kept Toots's correspondence relatively unchaotic for years, and on into the inner sanctum. There, Sherman gives Toots the news, the base on which Toots builds his philosophy for the day. If it is good news, Toots will have a ready conversation piece for his more cherished crums when they come in. If it is bad news, Toots will harbor it so as not to upset his friends who may be coming in to laugh. But, however bad, it will not crack his confidence that things will get better as the day wears on.

With that out of the way, Toots puts in phone calls to friends spread over the Eastern time zone. He doesn't start calling West Coast friends until midafternoon, for fear of awakening them. The calls are mostly neighborly: How are things? Where you been? Need anything? How about that Lombardy? How about that Mantle? How about . . . ? (Or there may be calls of greater substance: Hello, hello, honey

—See if you can find me a friend at Chase Manhattan. Then get me whatsisname, the headmaster at Rory's school.)

The calls are made against a remarkable backdrop that mutely speaks of Toots's life and times: a long table filled with the memorabilia of his varied life. There is LBJ staring at him appraisingly. There is Jack Kennedy, whom he adored, laughing with him; Gleason standing proudly in front of the cardboard Shor's he orders built when on location, and a relaxed Sinatra at the bar. A magnificent photographic study of Toots, in striped pants and sugar-shovel coat, stands with his beautiful Bari Ellen, taken at Kerry's wedding to stockbroker Jim Jacobson. And a jagged forest of cheap trophies and rusting plaques awarded to Toots for sundry forgotten achievements. The chairs, divan, and private washroom are littered with framed and unframed photos taken—usually by Toots's court photographer, Bill Mark—at parties, banquets, and special events reaching back to antebellum II. And big originals of the sports cartoons of Burris Jenkins, Jr., Willard Mullin, John Pierotti, and Tom Paprocki. Toots never got around to framing or mounting a remarkable and unquestionably valuable sketch of him by James Montgomery Flagg. ("He was a mean bastard, that bum was, but I'll say this for him. He did this of me at a party for Louise Baer, Bugs's wife. She was dying of heart trouble, but the sketch he made of her that night was the most beautiful thing you ever saw.")

Toots dictates letters after his morning phone calls. They are letters of thanks, further explorations into the recesses of friendship, letters forwarding a gift or good wishes. Such as:

MISS ESTHER SHOR
2101 Walnut Street
Philadelphia, Pa., 19103

DEAR ESTHER:
My friend, Bill Fugazy, has become President of the Diners Club and sent me an application for you to fill out so that you may become a member of the Diners Club. Please return it to me as soon as possible.
Just a quick note. Take care of yourself.
I love you.

                                                                    TOOTS

He gets replies, too:

THE WHITE HOUSE

WASHINGTON

February 4, 1969

DEAR TOOTS:

It was particularly gratifying to receive your good wishes following my Inauguration and I want you to know how deeply grateful I am.

Your prayers and your support will always be a source of inspiration and strength as I undertake the responsibility of providing new leadership for America in the years ahead.

With appreciation to you and your family from all the Nixons,

Sincerely,

DICK NIXON

Now it is time for him to face the throng downstairs. He makes no show of appearing on the scene. But his size, rolling gait, and his look—that of an outsized cherub returning to the heavenly host after a bad night in purgatory—command attention. He may walk past his oldest friend at the bar and barely acknowledge the fond greeting, while he gives the bar a fast head count. His first stop generally is at Klein's position under the archway leading into the restaurant portion. Sam gives him a quiet briefing on those present, those due, and why he is saving the corner table on the right.

The second-act curtain has gone up on the longest show in town. Toots will be on-stage until at least midnight and more often than not plunge into as many as four hours of the next day. He will have more speaking lines than his friend Richard Burton.

Over that period, a feat of great endurance, Toots will have a preluncheon bullshot or six with friends who must return to work around 2:30 P.M.; more drinks with regulars such as Paul Screvane, the Democrat, and Vince Albano, the Republican, and others who find it a nice place to spend an afternoon; and a drink to celebrate the arrival at 6 P.M. of trays of deep-fried little Swiss cheese and ham sandwiches—an item Toots picked up at Harry's Bar in Venice.

The dinner people drift in, some looking forward to having a drink with Toots. When they leave for their shows, there is time for Toots to have a drink with old chums and make calls to the West Coast. It is time for him to worry about Bob Hope's ailing eye, for example, or Phil Harris' liver, and to tell them over the phone to take care for crying out loud. By the time these errands of mercy are attended to, Toots suddenly realizes he hasn't eaten.

"Wanna eat?" he'll ask the one who is going the distance. If the crum says yes, they'll sit down and Toots will say, "Let's have a drink before dinner." He'll then look at a captain—Joe or Harry or young Ronnie—tap his empty brandy-and-soda with his stout right index finger and then make the little circles that mean he is sharing his liquid goods. Then he'll study the menu that has hardly changed since 1940.

"Look at that bum reading his own menu," a friend at another table once jeered. "That's like Moses restudying the Ten Commandments."

"I'll have . . . ," Toots will start, having assiduously studied the menu, apparently in search of flyspots. "I'll have . . . well, what've you got out there?" The captain sighs and recites everything Toots has just read. After perhaps ten minutes, Toots looks at the guy he's invited to dinner.

"Whatayagoingtohave?"

"Steak."

"I'll take the same," Toots will invariably say. The guy could have ordered snails with whipped cream smothered in Spam and Toots would have said, "I'll take the same."

By the time Toots has finished things off with a fruit Jello he is ready for the late crowd, or, more precisely, what is left of the late crowd. He blames television—"a monster"—and the roving muggers of Fun City for decimating what once was one of the liveliest and most profitable periods of the long day. He is wont to condemn the length of night baseball games, and he mourns the gradual extinction of the night-blooming New York sportswriter.

"On fight nights you couldn't get close to the bar," he laments. "Now all those sportswriters live in New Jersey or someplace like New Rochelle. Why, I remember when Frank Conniff had to take a house for Liz and the kids in New Rochelle, and commute, he never once bought a round-trip ticket when he left for New York. All he'd buy was a one-way, hoping something would happen and he wouldn't have to go back—and he could just send for the family. Now these young crums cover something at the Garden or a ball park and rush home for their malted milk and go to sleep, I guess. Show me ten of these new crums and I don't recognize but five or six. What's happening to the world?"

In the early morning hours, "fading" friends who dropped in around midnight to have a drink with him, Toots will say, looking around the empty dining room, "Pick 'em up." The captains will snap fingers at the sleepy busboys, who will move like an invasion of locusts through the room, turn the chairs upside down on the cleared tabletops so that their legs stick up like horns and their backrests hang like heavy beards over the edge of the tables. It gives a late, late patron the uneasy feeling that he is about to be gored by a stampede of yaks.

Toots and what's left of his court move to the depopulated bar, manned by now by Eddie Campis and Eddie Himmler. "Give us all a drink, Nazi," Toots will say, if it is Himmler he focuses on. Finally Himmler excuses himself. He must go home and get a little sleep before rushing to the track in time to bet the daily double.

"Let's go by P. J.'s and have one," Toots will sometimes say, if the long day and the longer night have been festive enough, or if he is with one of that Third Avenue bistro's habitués. Toots's car will be waiting without, without much in the way of splendor. It is an ostentatiously humble white Ford wagon, owned and operated by Sleepless Sol, a faithful man. It is never difficult to locate among the purring Cadillacs, Continentals, and Rolls-Royces lined up waiting for the late Twenty-one crowd to emerge.

Sol waits at P. J.'s for Toots, then takes him home along the nearly empty streets of Manhattan. Athletes half Toots's age and considerably sounder of wind have collapsed under this regimen and lain abed until the next noon, pondering the rigors of going the distance. But Toots must be up and stirring three hours before that. He must get to the store to "see some guys" and confront another day that's bound to be better.

One recent afternoon Bill Slocum dropped into Toots's and Toots wasn't visible or audible.

"He caught a beaut today," Sam Klein explained. "He's home resting. See Rory?"

"Little Toots" was sitting at one of the tables in the bar. He is becoming a dead-ringer for the Toots who charged out of South Philadelphia forty years ago. He's acquiring the muscular build Toots once had. He has the dimples, the curly blond hair, the blue eyes, and, fortuitously, his mother's manners. He wants to go to work "in the back" and begin his apprenticeship. But Toots is determined to keep him in school so long that the college will graduate him and make him its president at the same ceremony.

Slocum sat down next to his young friend who, though temporarily flat-pocket, was just finishing a split of imported champagne. Rory looked up at Sam and tapped the lip of his glass with his index finger. Then he made a little circle in the air.

Slocum sighed.

"Dear God," he said, "here we go again."

Index

Adams, Franklin P., 181
Addie, Bob, 66, 144
Adonis, Joe, 142, 177, 178
Adrian, Iris, 36
Albano, Vince, 205
Allen, Fred, 39, 120
Ameche, Don, 80, 97, 99, 101
Annapolis, Md., 174
Arcaro, Eddie, 97, 172
Atlantic City, N.J., 14, 16, 17, 25, 28, 38, 108

Bachman, Mark, 33
Baer, Buddy, 182
Baer, Bugs, 2, 120, 172
Baer, Louise, 204
Baer, Max, 14, 182
Bainbridge, John, 70, 169
Baldino, Lou, 108
Barbara, Lou, 61
Barber, Red, 73
Barr, Phil, 38, 39
Barrow, Ed, 174
Barry, Jack, 95, 96, 200, 203
Barry, Tom, 32
Baruch, Bernard, 135
Beaverbrook, Lord, 138
Beck, Leonard, 85, 86
Bennett, Jean, 189
Benny, Jack, 34, 109
Bergen, Edgar, 41
Bernhart, Joe, 24
Berns (21 Club), 51, 146
Berra, Yogi, 1, 113, 134, 148, 187
Berstein, Will, 43
Big Frenchy, *see* La Mange, George
Billingsley, Sherman, 24, 25, 26, 27, 32, 33, 47, 49, 51, 52, 82, 94, 97, 98, 99, 100, 101, 102
Bishop, Jim, 164
Blair, Nicky, 36, 94, 144
Boggiano, Johnny, 45
Boonville, Mo., 73, 74, 76, 77
Boston, Sam, 37
Brisson, Carl, 98

Broderick, Bob, 95, 188–189, 200, 203
Broderick, Johnny, 31, 99, 177
Buchwald, Art, 134
Buck, Al, 71
Budge, Don, 172
Burns, George, 26
Burton, Richard, 205
Byron, Ed, 64

Cagney, Jimmy, 25
Cahn, Sammy, 196
Campis, Eddie, 207
Cannon, Jimmy, 45, 53, 117, 151, 166, 187, 190
Canzoneri, Tony, 103
Capdell, Poms, 115
Carroll, Earl, 25, 36
Carver, Lawton, 92, 144
Casserly, Jack, 136, 137
Cerf, Bennett, 181
Champlin, Charles, 113, 119
Chandler, Albert B. (Happy), 82
Chaplin, Charlie, 67
Chicago, Ill., 23, 31, 95
Christo, Mr., 24, 27
Churchill, Randolph, 111
Clark, Wilbur, 179
Clifford, Clark, 146, 201
Cohen, Jack, 24
Coleman, Emil, 34
Coleman, Tom, 202
Coll, Pete, 31
Coll, Vincent (Mad Dog), 31
Collins, Jimmy, 35
Colonna, Jerry, 201
Compton, Betty, 176
Conerly, Charley, 198
Conn, Billy, 82, 83, 85, 148, 201
Conniff, Frank, 71, 74, 75, 97, 99, 193, 207
Conniff, Liz, 207
Connolly, Joseph V., 176, 177
Connors, Lefty, 5
Considine, Bob, 94

Conzelman, Jimmy, 76, 182
Cooke, Jack Kent, 145
Corum, Bill, 26, 27, 37, 42, 47, 48, 51, 66, 73, 74, 76, 77, 79, 80, 81, 82, 84, 97, 98, 99, 120, 145, 166, 168, 191
Corum, Clayton, 74
Corum, Mrs. (Mom), 74, 75, 76, 77, 168
Costello, Frank, 1, 177, 178, 179, 180
Cronkite, Walter, 187, 201
Crosby, Bing, 25, 26, 109
Cross and Dunn, 40, 52

Dalitz, Moe, 179
Daly, John, 134, 136, 148, 174, 198, 201
Davis, Eddie, 34, 36, 37, 39, 91, 109, 121, 146, 186, 187
Davis, Phil, 35
Day, A. Grove, 168
Deal, N. J., 60, 83
Dean, Barney, 26
DeMarco, Renée, 34
DeMarco, Tony, 34, 40
Demaret, Jimmy, 172
Dempsey, Jack, 31, 47, 50, 93, 148, 187, 192, 195
Dickey, Bill, 173
DiMaggio, Dom, 175
DiMaggio, Joe, 65, 79, 82, 116, 139, 172, 173, 174, 175
DiMaggio, Vince, 65
Donahue, Mrs. Woolworth, 26
Donald, Peter, 148
Douglas, Paul, 63, 112, 113
Dowling, Eddie, 25, 27, 29
Draper, Paul, 1, 181
Dubinsky, David, 176
Dubow, Lou, 176
Duchin, Eddy, 49, 80, 175
Dunn, Henry, 52; see also Cross and Dunn
Durante, Jimmy, 80, 165
Durgom, Bullets, 64
Durocher, Leo, 110, 116, 173
Dwyer, Bill, 31
Dykes, Jimmy, 174

Eckert, William D. (Spike), 82
Edward VIII, 4
Edwards, Ralph, 105, 106, 107, 108, 109, 110, 111
Eisenhower, Dwight David, 164, 199
Ellis Island, N.Y., 4

Enken, Leon, 34, 35, 36, 37, 38, 39, 91, 109, 121, 146, 186, 187
Erdelatz, Eddie, 174
Ernie, Val, 35

Fadiman, Clifton, 24, 181
Fairless, Ben, 77
Falkenberg, Jinx, 105, 108, 111, 172, 173
Farley, Jim, 148, 175
Farnsworth, Bill, 37, 91
Feder, Sid, 167
Feller, Bobby, 148
Fisher, Eddie, 69
Flagg, James Montgomery, 204
Flaherty, Vincent X., 66
Flanagan, Dick, 94
Fleming, Sir Alexander, 1
Flippen, J. C., 26, 52
Florence, Italy, 135
Folsom, Frank, 68
Fonseca, Lew, 149
Ford, Whitey, 87, 134, 148, 150, 187, 198
Fowler, Gene, 42, 165, 166
Frick, Ford, 82, 112, 114, 148
Froelich, Charles, 50, 51
Fugazy, Bill, 204

Galbreath, John, 86, 87
Galento, Tony, 48, 49
Gibbons, Harold, 146, 147
Gibbs, Ed, 194
Gilmartin, Joe, 11
Glad, Gladys, 35
Gleason, Jackie, 34, 43–44, 61, 62, 63, 64, 69, 110, 120, 137, 148, 149, 171, 186–187, 192, 199, 204
Goldman, Mrs. Aaron C., 100
Goldwyn, Sam, 90
Golenpaul, Dan, 181
Gomez, Lefty, 175
Gordon, Waxie, 31
Graham, Billy, 92, 93
Graham, Frank, 173
Gransky, Mr., 33
Grant, Arnold, 87, 100, 102, 143, 144
Graziano, Rocky, 172
Greenberg, Max, 31
Guinan, Texas, 1, 27
Guinan, Tommy, 27

Halley, Rudy, 179
Hannagan, Steve, 51
Hannegan, Bob, 183, 184

Harriman, W. Averell, 172
Harrington, Pat, 34, 69
Harris, Curly, 63, 192, 193
Harris, Phil, 148, 206
Harrison, Joe, 69, 95
Harron, Paul, 44, 45, 46, 48
Hawkins, Bert, 144
Hayes, Teddy, 47
Hearst, Bill, Jr., 78
Hellinger, Mark, 2, 26, 27, 32, 33, 35, 36, 42, 47, 94 120, 138, 175, 191
Hellinger, Mrs. Mark, 35
Hemingway, Ernest, 61, 169, 170, 171
Henie, Sonja, 200
Henrich, Tommy, 173
Hickman, Herman, 77
Hill, Virginia, 180
Himmler, Eddie, 207
Hines, Jimmy, 37
Hoffa, Jimmy, 2, 146, 147
Hogan, Ben, 78, 175
Hoover, J. Edgar, 134, 201
Hope, Bob, 2, 26, 78, 94, 165, 196, 201, 206
Hope, Delores, 94, 201
Hopkins, Harry, 171
Horn, George, 47, 48
Horne, Lena, 141
Hot Springs, Ark., 60, 180
Hubbell, Carl, 172
Hughes, Howard, 92, 178
Humphrey, Hubert, 201
Husing, Ted, 67
Hyers, Frankie, 34
Hyman, Dick, 173

Impelliteri, Vincent, 78

Jacobs, Mike, 82
Jacobson, Jim, 204
Jacobson, Mrs. Jim, see Shor, Kerry
Janeway, Elizabeth, 182
Jenkins, Burris, Jr., 204
Jessel, George, 14, 26, 40, 72, 96, 148
Johansson, Ingemar, 170
John XXIII (Pope), 137
Johnson, Lady Bird, 201
Johnson, Lyndon, 104, 201, 204
Jolson, Al, 109
Justin, Leo, 2, 45, 48, 50, 51, 66, 72, 85, 94, 121, 143

Kannen, Harry, 39, 40, 41
Karr, Joe, 12, 13–14, 15
Kastell, Phil, 178, 179
Kaufman, Bill (Pop), 17
Kaufman, Dewey, 16
Kearns, Jack, 93
Kelly, Bradley, 147
Kelly, Jimmy (Flatnose), 6, 11
Kelly, Shipwreck, 172
Kennedy, John F., 72, 145, 196, 204
Kennedy, Joseph P., 191
Kennedy, Robert F., 2, 145, 191, 201
Kieran, John, 181
Kilgallen, Dorothy, 70
Kintner, Robert, 201
Klein, Rabbi, 7
Klein, Sam, 200, 203, 205, 208
Kriendler (21 Club), 51, 146, 148
Krompier, Marty, 31
Kuhn, Bowie, 82
Kupcinet, Irving, 165

LaHiff, Billy, 42, 139
LaHiff, Billy, Jr., 44
La Mange, George (Big Frenchy), 1, 24–25, 26, 28, 30, 32, 39, 40
Lamaze, George, 26
Landis, Kenesaw Mountain, 81, 82
Lardner, Ring, 42, 67
Larsen, Don, 112, 113
Las Vegas, Nev., 92, 96, 178
Layden, Elmer, 37
Lefkowitz, Louis, 148
Leipzig, Germany, 4
Lescoulie, Jack, 64
Levy, Ike, 44
Lewis, Joe E., 17, 38, 44, 96, 105, 195, 201
Lewis, Patricia, 138, 139, 140
Libuse, Frank, 93
Logan, Ella, 93
London, England, 137, 138
Louchheim, Jerry, 26
Loughran, Tommy, 9
Louis, Joe, 78–79, 82, 83, 139, 172, 182
Louisville, Ky., 97, 98
Lucas, Charlie, 33, 34
Luciano, Charlie (Lucky), 31, 39, 40, 142, 167, 177
Luckman, Charles, 149, 190, 191
Lyons, Leonard, 137, 182

MacArthur, Douglas, 172
McCarthy, Eugene, 201
McCormack, Bill, 192, 193

McDonald, Bill, 144, 145
McGraw, John, 174
McGuigan, Jack, 11
McIntyre, Marvin, 183
Madden, Owney, 1, 24, 27, 28, 29,
    30, 31, 32, 60, 179
Maglie, Sal, 112
Mandel, Jack, 41
Mann, Arthur, 74, 166
Mantle, Mickey, 87, 134, 148, 191
March, Hal, 112
Marciano, Rocky, 172, 188
Mark, Bill, 204
Marshall, George Preston, 145–146
Martin, Billy, 191
Marx, Groucho, 187, 188
Maxwell, Elsa, 181
Mayer, Louis B., 66, 67
Meadows, Audrey, 172
Meany, Tom, 173, 174
Menjou, Adolph, 27
Merman, Ethel, 68, 80
Meyers, Lee, 64, 74, 148
Michener, James A., 168
Moore, Terry, 82
Morgan, Helen, 39
Morse, Robert, 187
Mosconi, Willie, 65
Moss, Joe, 24
Mullin, Willard, 204
Munich, Germany, 4
Murrow, Edward R., 1, 69
Musial, Stan, 76, 165

Nadler, Teddy, 111, 112, 113
Nettie, 29–30
Newman, Doc, 177
Newman, Frances Moody, 140
Newman, Gus, 140
Newsom, Bobo, 120
New York, N. Y., 1, 17, 23, 33, 141
Nick and Arnold, 40, 41
Nielsen, Grace, 203
Nixon, Richard, 205
North, John Ringling, 101
Nova, Lou, 48, 49
Noyes, Charles F., 47, 48, 85
Nunan, Catherine, 68
Nunan, Joe, 68, 86, 94

O'Brien, Hugh, 188
O'Brien, Larry, 201
O'Brien, Pat, 110, 167, 198
O'Donnell, Leo, 7
O'Donnell, Rosy, 71
O'Dwyer, Bill, 148

Onassis, Aristotle, 194
O'Reilly, Tom, 120

Padua, Italy, 135
Palm Beach, Fla., 4, 103
Paprocki, Tom, 204
Paris, France, 136, 137
Patterson, Floyd, 170
Paul VI (Pope), 3, 199
Pearl, Jack, 39, 70
Pearl, Mrs. Jack, 70
Philadelphia, Pa., 1, 6, 16, 26, 28,
    36, 45, 48, 84, 97, 141; see also
    South Philadelphia
Piermont, Sidney, 40, 45, 52
Pierotti, John, 204
Porter, Paul, 201
Povich, Shirley, 66, 144
Pulley, B. S., 44
Pyle, Ernie, 172

Ragland, Rags, 63, 69, 78, 95, 181,
    183
Reilly, Terry, 42
Reynolds, James, 184, 201
Reynolds, Quentin, 94, 105, 106,
    114, 116, 165, 166, 184
Rice, Grantland, 120, 165, 191
Richman, Harry, 25
Rifkind, Simon, 101, 102
Rizzuto, Phil, 113
Robinson, Murray, 138, 139
Robinson, Wilbert, 174
Rocky (N. J. boss), 15
Rogers, Donald I., 188
Rogers, William P., 201
Rome, Italy, 135, 136
Rooney, Art, 168
Roosevelt, Franklin D., 24, 72, 120,
    171, 183, 184
Ross, Barney, 103, 104
Ross, Lillian, 169
Rote, Kyle, 148
Runyon, Damon, 139
Rusk, Howard, 201
Russell, Fred, 165
Ruth, Babe, 1, 74, 78, 120, 137–138
Ruth, Clair, 137, 138

St. Louis, Mo., 73, 74
St. Petersburg, U.S.S.R., 4
Schmidt, Francis, 37
Schulman, Arnold, 65
Schultz, Dutch, 27, 31
Schumacher, Garry, 75, 76
Scott, Irving, 50

Screvane, Paul, 205
Sears, Grad, 51, 66, 71
Shannon, Ireland, 135
Sherman, Charlie, 27, 32
Sherman, Dick, 89, 90, 189, 202, 203
Sherman, Irving, 48
Sherwood, Robert, 1, 120, 170, 171, 172, 173
Shor, Abraham, 1, 3, 4, 6, 7, 8, 9, 10, 11, 12, 107
Shor, Bari Ellen, 37, 70, 81, 94, 110, 111, 112, 113, 183, 204
Shor, Bertha, 3, 8, 9, 10, 12, 13, 14, 27
Shor, Esther, 3, 7, 8, 9, 12, 13, 27, 107, 204
Shor, Fanny Kaufman, 1, 3, 4, 6, 7, 8–9, 14, 107
Shor, Kerry, 45, 86, 110, 184, 194, 199, 204
Shor, Marian Volk (Baby; Husky), 36, 37, 38, 39, 41, 42, 45, 46, 47, 48, 53, 60, 68, 70, 72, 73, 81, 84, 88, 89, 93, 97, 98, 109, 111, 112, 117, 121, 134, 135, 136, 151, 165, 166, 168, 175, 177, 179, 182, 183, 184, 190, 194
Shor, Rory, 111, 114, 115, 148, 204, 208
Siegel, Benny, 177, 178
Siegel, Moe, 144
Silvers, Phil, 65, 148
Sinatra, Frank, 78, 80, 94, 139, 183, 196, 198, 199, 204
Skelton, Red, 203
Sleepless Sol (chauffeur), 207
Slocum, Bill, 149, 208
Slocum, Frank, 111, 112
Small, Paul, 41
Smith, Red, 114
Sobol, Louis, 70
Solomon, Sid, 175
South Philadelphia, 1, 4, 9, 14, 107, 165, 208
Spellman, Francis Cardinal, 1, 148, 164, 191, 199
Spiro, Amster, 37
Spooner, Jack, 43
Steinberg, John, 24, 27
Stengel, Casey, 1, 137, 196
Stern, Philip Van Doren, 100
Stevens, Frank, 48
Stokowski, Leopold, 181
Stoneham, Horace, 47, 67, 75, 91, 94
Street, Ben, 16
Sullivan, Ed, 42, 70, 148

Sullivan, Jerry, 30
Sutton, Lou, 25
Sutton, Willie, 165
Swope, Herbert Bayard, 202
Symington, Stuart, 201

Taft, Robert A., 185
Talley, Truman, 52
Terry, Bill, 43
Thorpe, Sam, 41
Tobey, Charles W., 179
Todd, Mike, 182
Topping, Mr. and Mrs. Dan, 200
Tracy, Bob, 83
Tracy, Matt, 83, 84, 85, 103
Truman, Harry S., 1, 171, 172, 184, 185
Truman, Margaret, 172, 185
Tunney, Gene, 67

Vallee, Rudy, 41
Vance Sisters, 34
Vandenberg, Arthur H., 185
Van Doren, Charles, 24
Van Heusen, Jimmy, 196
Veeck, Bill, 165
Venice, Italy, 135
Venturi, Ken, 104
Vitullo, Gus, 9, 10
Volk, Ethel O'Shea, 36, 73, 180
Volk, John, 36

Waldron, Jack, 195
Walker, Jimmy, 23, 31, 42, 71, 120, 166, 175, 176, 177
Walker, Mrs. Jimmy, 176
Warren, Earl, 1, 134, 142, 148, 149, 186, 201
Warren, Virginia, 134, 142
Washington, D.C., 183, 184, 200, 201
Wayne, John, 194
Webb, Del, 178
Weiss, George, 174
Weiss, Mr., 33
Weiss, Rudy, 24, 35
Weiss, Seymour, 96
Welles, Orson, 142
Wheeler, Bert, 68
White, George, 25
White, Jack, 34
Whitney, Jock, 27, 87
Wilkes-Barre, Pa., 15, 16
Williams, Edward Bennett, 166, 180, 201
Williams, Joe, 169

Williams, Ted, 65
Wilson, Earl, 61, 134, 137, 165, 187,
    198
Winchell, Walter, 27, 33, 42
Windsor, Duke of, *see* Edward VIII
Wismer, Harry, 67, 144
Wynn, Ed, 79

Yacht Club Boys, 34
Yawkey, Tom, 48

Zeckendorf, Bill, 87, 88, 89, 113,
    143, 146
Zeibert, Duke, 144, 145
Ziegfeld, Florenz, 25
Zimbalist, Sam, 182
Zurich, Switzerland, 136
Zwillman, Abner (Longy), 1, 177,
    179, 180, 181
Zwillman, Mrs. Abner, 179